More Praise for *Living a Life on Loan*

Christians definitely need reminding that we are saved *from* something *for* something. I am grateful to God for raising up Rick and Eric to do just that. This book is a much-needed call to the church to join God in what Paul Harvey would call "the rest of the story." I heartily endorse this book!

—RICK ATCHLEY, Richland Hills Church of Christ,
North Richland Hills, Texas

Say yes to life as it was meant to be—learn from *Living a Life on Loan.* You, and your small group, could be transformed . . . for all eternity!

—BOB RUSSELL, Southeast Christian Church, Louisville, Kentucky

Rick Rusaw is the most intuitive leader I know. The stories and ideas in this book will help you think in new ways about the ministry of reconciliation to which we all have been called.

—PAUL S. WILLIAMS, president, Orchard Group, Inc.;
editor-at-large, *Christian Standard*

Our lives are not really ours. Rick and Eric offer sound guidance for investing wisely what we cannot keep.

—JOHN ORTBERG, author of *If You Want to Walk on Water,
You've Got to Get Out of the Boat*

Most of us need help thinking through the daily practicalities of living our heavenly citizenship right here in the muck and mire of planet Earth. Rick Rusaw and Eric Swanson have done us all a great service by translating the abstract into the concrete.

—RUBEL SHELLY, Woodmont Hills Church of Christ,
Nashville, Tennessee

The tragedy of all tragedies is to come to the end of life, look back, and feel as though we wasted precious time and important opportunities. This book offers the keys to making every moment count, living life to its fullest, and being a faithful steward of all that God has given us.

—DUDLEY C. RUTHERFORD, Shepherd of the Hills Church, Porter Ranch, California

Living a Life on Loan reminds us that our lives are not as much a gift we have received as they are a gift we give. This book is a must-read for those of us who want Christ to be reflected both in our creeds and in our deeds.

—DR. ELI MORRIS, Hope Church, Memphis, Tennessee

Living a Life on Loan is practical and pertinent. Rick and Eric have a way of motivating me to stop looking in the mirror and start serving others.

—DAVE STONE, Southeast Christian Church, Louisville, Kentucky

Living a Life on Loan makes you think and brings stewardship to a new level: my life is not mine; it's God's life on loan to me. The book graciously takes you down a path to review the moments of your life and answer the question "What does God want from me?" He wants it ALL!

—DR. ROBERT C. VARNEY, Campus Crusade for Christ International

LIVING A LIFE ON LOAN

LIVING A **LIFE** ON LOAN™

Finding Grace at the Intersections

RICK RUSAW AND ERIC SWANSON

Standard®
PUBLISHING
Bringing The Word to Life

Cincinnati, Ohio

Published by Standard Publishing, Cincinnati, Ohio

www.standardpub.com

Printed in the United States of America

Jacket and interior design: The DesignWorks Group

Editorial assistance: Krista Petty

LIBRARY OF CONGRESS CATALOGING-IN-PUBLICATION DATA:

Rusaw, Rick, 1959-

Living a life on loan : finding grace at the intersections / Rick Rusaw and Eric Swanson.

    p. cm.

ISBN 0-7847-1855-5

1. Christian life. 2. Stewardship, Christian. I. Swanson, Eric, 1950- II. Title.

BV4501.3.R865 2006

248.4--dc22

2005037910

12 11 10 09 08 07   9 8 7 6 5 4 3 2

DEDICATION

To my dad and mom, Boyd and Violet Swanson—
now in their eighties, from the greatest generation—
still so full of life and so full of love,
who modeled for me the meaning
of living a life on loan.
And to my son, Jeff,
who is overseas fighting for a people's right to live free;
to his courageous wife, Ashlie;
and to my first grandchild, Gentry David Swanson.

—E. S.

A portion of my parents' story is recorded in these pages.
I have watched as two people have dealt with tragedy,
disappointment, and the harsh realities of life—
yet have chosen to live beyond their heartaches. Their lives
are marked by love, generosity, and grace.
While many have the privilege of calling you their friends,
I get to call you Mom and Dad.
If there were a gate to stand and applaud at, I would.
Thanks for your love, for your example of grace, and for
allowing God to write his story through you.
A special thanks to my wife, Diane, whose generous spirit
and love for me is a gift that lights my life.

—R. R.

CONTENTS

INTRODUCTION

There are people who prefer to say "Yes," and there
are people who prefer to say "No." Those who say "Yes"
are rewarded by the adventures they have, and those who say
"No" are rewarded by the safety they attain.

—KEITH JOHNSTONE

Every adventure begins when we say yes. No adventure has ever begun with the words "I think I'll pass on this one" or "Call me next month when my schedule lightens up." Every great voyage of discovery began with people who wanted more than safety—they wanted adventure. In the early 1900s, when Sir Ernest Shackleton was looking for a crew to man the *Endurance* on his journey to the South Pole, he put the following advertisement in the papers of London:

> Men wanted for hazardous journey. Small wages. Bitter cold. Long months of complete darkness. Constant danger. Safe return doubtful. Honour and recognition in case of success.[1]

Five thousand men applied for the job. They said yes to the adventure that awaited them.

Living life as it was meant to be lived begins by saying yes. When was the last time you gave a resounding "Yes!" to life, to the adventure that awaits you, and to God? Living a life on loan requires that you say yes.

A LIFE NOT YOUR OWN

A life on loan—like every loan—is given with the expectation of a return. We are to return more than we are given. One day we will be held accountable for how we spent or invested our lives. Life begins with—and belongs to—God. Though we often speak of life and all it comprises as gifts from God, they are unique "gifts" in that, technically, they still belong to him.

The Bible says, "The earth is the LORD's, and everything in it, the world, and all who live in it" (Psalm 24:1). You belong to God. The life you live comes from him alone. One of Jesus' followers expressed it this way: "You are not your own; you were bought at a price" (1 Corinthians 6:19, 20).

And this life on earth does not last forever. Jesus said, "Who of you by worrying can add a single hour to his life?" (Matthew 6:27). You have a span of days that God gives you to accomplish what he has placed you on earth to do. It is up to you to use well the time you've been given.

Begin thinking of your life as *on loan* rather than as a life *you own*. If you own something, you are free to give it away, sell it, or exchange it with whomever you choose. But if your life belongs to someone else and is on loan to you, that changes everything. Before you give your life (or even portions of it) away, you have to check with the owner first.

WHAT IS LIFE?

Jesus gives just enough hints to let us know that life can be defined . . . that real life can be discovered. He said, "I came that they might have life, and might have it abundantly" (John 10:10, *NASB*) and,

"A man's life does not consist in the abundance of his possessions" (Luke 12:15). If life isn't about what we own, then what *is* it about? What does real life look like? What does God want in return for the life he has loaned each of us? That's what this book is all about.

We've created an acrostic for the word *life* to help us remember what life consists of: Loves, Intersections, Fortune, and Eternity. Treating each of these components of life as God directs is the way to live a life on loan.

Loves

What you love is seen in your passions, your purpose, your priorities, and your values. The love Jesus spoke of involved "heart and . . . soul and . . . mind" (Matthew 22:37)—a love that goes beyond emotion and involves action, rationale, and intellect. Whom you love includes the people in your life and God. Understanding your loves is foundational for living a life on loan.

Intersections

If your life has intersected with God, he is influencing your story; and if you are intersecting with others, he wants to influence them through you. God places you alongside others so that your story intersects with their stories in such a way that God's story becomes part of their stories. It was a slave who influenced many in Caesar's household to come to faith (Philippians 4:22). It was a mere wine taster living in Babylon who influenced a king to repatriate a country (Nehemiah 1:11; 2:8). When you demonstrate the love of Christ in practical ways, you'll earn the right to tell others what motivates your service. And when your stories intersect . . . grace happens.

Fortune

All of us have resources that come to us in the form of a loan from God. Whether you began life with more or less, you have some amount of fortune and can invest your fortune to accomplish God's purposes both in your life and in the lives of others. God can accomplish much with people who may have only meager resources but who have big hearts. The impoverished widow who gave her two small copper coins is commended for what she did with her "fortune" (see Luke 21:1-4).

Eternity

Picture yourself back in high school geometry class. The teacher begins at one end of the board and draws a line to the other end. But this line really begins before that one end of the board. And it goes on forever; it really continues past the board, out the window, over the ball field, through the parking lot, into the subdivision, over the open space, into the mountains, and then, accounting for the curvature of the earth, off into space where it might eventually pierce a few distant stars.

Eternity is like that line—without beginning or end. Along that line of eternity, your life would best be represented by a small dot. Stepping away from the line, you would probably conclude, "Life is very short . . . and eternity is very loooooooooooooong." What if it were possible to think about living your life in relation to the line and not simply the dot? What if God has structured life in such a way that the things you do in this dot could influence all of eternity? One day you'll stand before God—the one who loaned you your life. If you want to hear him say "Well done!" then you want to prove faithful with your dot of time.

SAY YES TO LIFE

A few months ago a friend and I (Eric) were walking along the Pearl Street Mall in Boulder, Colorado, on the way to lunch. A friendly panhandler (rude panhandling is outlawed in Boulder) approached us with a very clever line: "Hey, buddy, could you loan me a couple of bucks? I'm trying to raise a down payment on a cheeseburger." We had a good laugh together and took him to lunch with us. The panhandler got more than he'd hoped for. We'd like to think that's a bit what God is like. You ask him for a simple loan, and he gives you a wonderful, many-faceted gift.

In the chapters that follow, we'll explain more about what it means to live your life as on loan from God, and we'll introduce you to people whose stories are intersecting with the story God is weaving throughout history. You'll meet some very ordinary people who are cutting a big swath for the kingdom of God, and perhaps you'll find your story in their stories. Our prayer is that, by the end of this book, you will be among those who are living their lives on loan.

Being indebted to God is a good thing. There's a saying that goes something like this: "If you owe a man a hundred dollars, you've got a problem. But if you owe a man a million dollars, then *he's* got a problem." You owe God way more than millions of dollars, and he gladly accepts that as *his* problem. He will do everything he can, moving Heaven and earth, to see that you don't default on this loan. Why? Because it's in your best interest! And it will all come back to him, along with a wonderful return. He'll work with you to help you succeed in bringing back way more than he ever gave you.

We write this book not merely to provide information and inspiration but for reflection *and* action. Action without reflection is thoughtless, but reflection without action is nearly useless. We believe that as you read *Living a Life on Loan*, you will be reading two books. The first is the book composed of the words we've written, and the second is the one composed of the thoughts and reflections God brings to mind and entrusts to you. At the end of each chapter, we'll pose a few questions. We've entitled the question section "What About You?" Take your time and reflect on what you have read. Additionally, in the back of the book, we've provided several blank pages for you to write your reflections and action steps as you read. Of the two books in your hand, the one *you* write is the more important one.

LOVES

There are 66 books in the Bible, 1,189 chapters, 31,101 verses, and 783,137 words. In the Old Testament and New Testament there are 6,468 commands to obey. The Bible can be read aloud in about seventy hours.[1] That's a lot of Scripture and a lot of reading time. Thankfully, Jesus gives us a CliffsNotes summary of all of Scripture in Matthew 22:37-40 where he says, "'Love the Lord your God with all your heart and with all your soul and with all your mind.' This is the first and greatest commandment. And the second is like it: 'Love your neighbor as yourself.' All the Law and the Prophets hang on these two commandments."

The Bible teaches us how to live in loving relationships with God and with other people. John writes, "Love comes from God" (1 John 4:7) and, "We love because he first loved us" (1 John 4:19). Love is one of those special gifts on loan from God. Our ability to love God, our neighbor, and even our enemies (see Matthew 5:43, 44) comes from him. Authentic love for God and others expresses itself through our identity, our values, and our purpose.

1

YOUR STORY MATTERS

The question to ask at the end of life's race

is not so much "What have I accomplished?"

but "Whom have I loved, and how courageously?"

—GEOFF GORSUCH

News anchor Peter Jennings was a man who loved telling people's stories. It was said that while on assignment in foreign countries, he sometimes put his hand over his eyes, placed a finger on the map, and told his crew, "Let's go find the story there." While waiting for a special event or for an interview with a famous person, he went to find the story of the common person.

Everyone has a story. If a famous reporter showed up at your door, what would your story be? What events have defined your life until now?

ONCE UPON A TIME

My (Rick's) grandmother on my mom's side ran away and joined the circus at a very young age. In case you didn't know, life under the big top is a tough career path! My grandmother was one of those ladies who spun around on a big wheel while knives were thrown at her. My grandmother's decision to join the circus was just one in a series of bad choices that she made for herself and her children. Long before it was culturally popular, she had lived with plenty of guys. She was married a number of times and didn't actually divorce as many times as she was married. My grandmother also had a problem with alcohol. My mom remembers being taken to a bar one night when she was four and her brother was only two. They spent the bulk of the night there, and a stranger ended up taking them home because my grandmother couldn't be found. That pattern was repeated over and over again. Grandmother would show up sometimes for six weeks, or six months, and then dump my mom and her brother off someplace again.

The plot thickens

My grandmother's story is sad, and my mom's began with even more sadness. Mom grew up in and out of foster homes. She met her biological father only one time that she can remember. At one point in her story, though, there was a light in the darkness: a loving family that tried to remain in contact with her, attempting to be a stable presence in her life.

At the same time my mom was drifting in and out of foster homes, another story was being written across town. By the time my dad was in eighth grade, he had moved fourteen times. One of his grandfathers helped construct the state prison in upstate New York, and his other grandfather lived in it when it was completed. It was always difficult for my dad's side of the family to have a reunion because they had trouble getting parole dates to coincide. As you can imagine, my dad's family, like my mom's, had lots of issues! Dad ended up quitting school in eighth grade. After a few years of odd jobs, he started working for a pharmaceutical company. He made a decision to stick with that job, no matter how tough or boring it got, and eventually he landed a management position, earned a GED, and worked toward a college degree—all because he made a decision that was a significant break from a long-standing family pattern.

My mom and dad ended up being next-door neighbors, but their families had little regard for each other. Eventually they became a young couple and got married when they were only nineteen. Even with nobody to show them the way, my parents made one important decision that changed the way their stories were being written. They decided that they were not going to be like their families; they were going to make different choices, provide a stable home for their kids, and find their own way. To do that, they knew they needed to move away. They began taking weekend trips to drive around the suburbs of Syracuse, New York, looking for a place to rent or maybe even buy someday. They didn't have much money and no means of purchasing their home, but that didn't stop them from dreaming about it.

Happily ever after

Time passed. One weekend while driving and dreaming, they stopped at a real estate open house and met Clayton, a realtor, who wound up driving my parents to look at houses that afternoon. They eventually got around to telling him their story and admitting they really didn't have money for a down payment. Clayton, who was nearing retirement, said that he really wanted to help them get a good start—a better start than they had already been given. After consulting with his wife, he personally loaned them the money to make a down payment. Mom and Dad loaded up my sister and me, and we moved into a new home—away from the pains of the past. On the first of every month for nearly seven years, Dad put us all into the car and drove to Clayton's to make a payment on the loan.

About the same time that we moved into our new neighborhood, a preacher named Jerry and his wife, Judy, left New Jersey to help with a small new church in Liverpool, New York. While Jerry worked at the church, he also worked part-time driving a school bus. Jerry and Judy lived in the house right behind the church building and, with their young children, found ways to be involved in the life of the neighborhood. Jerry often tried to visit the families living there. Whenever he came to our door, I thought it was a game because as soon as the doorbell rang, Mom or Dad would say, "Everyone keep quiet!" Though my parents had made some choices to improve our family's future, they didn't go to church—and they weren't about to start.

Though my parents had made some choices to improve our family's future, they didn't go to church— and they weren't about to start.

One of the best ways Jerry found to connect with people was to pay attention to my friends and me who used the churchyard as a sports field. Sometimes he helped us mow yard markers or foul lines into the grass; sometimes he helped settle our fights or resolve a situation when we'd broken a window. He also rescued our baseballs from the grouchy neighbor who took the balls that rolled into his yard and wouldn't give them back without a major confrontation. We all thought Jerry was a pretty nice guy.

Though some of us were a little rough around the edges, Jerry invited us to go to church camp, and I discovered faith and a relationship with Christ at that camp. It wasn't long before my parents also discovered faith. They were willing to overlook some of their hurts of the past and share their faith with my grandparents. Over time, some aunts, uncles, and cousins discovered God's grace. Both sides of my family found that it was not too late to write new endings to their stories.

That's some of my story. What's yours?

WHAT'S YOUR STORY?

Your name identifies you, but it doesn't necessarily describe who you are. Let's suppose you are speeding down the road and see the lights of a police car flashing in your mirror. You pull over, and the officer comes to your car and asks for your name. Your name provides recognition and identification, but it can't provide insight as to who you are and why you were speeding. It's your *story* that tells others who you are.

We've met people whose stories mimic a Greek tragedy and seem doomed from the start, while others seem to have a fairy tale beginning. But no matter how your story begins, you are responsible for writing the *ending*. Most people either blame or credit their family trees for the way their stories go. I don't have far to climb in my own family tree to share both tragedy and fairy tale. My parents are both incredible people who had to overcome some very difficult times. While my dad's family put the fun in dys*fun*ctional, my mom's family took it out. How did each of their stories go from tragedy to triumph? The direction changed moment by moment as they allowed themselves to be written into a bigger story—God's story.

I am so grateful for a number of people who loved me and helped direct my story, even before I knew it: the family that compassionately always tried to find my mom when she was in foster care, the guy who gave my dad a job, the realtor who sacrificially lent my parents money, and the preacher who gladly took a chance with the boys who broke windows. Without realtor Clayton's generosity, we would not have been in that neighborhood. While we don't know what life might have looked like or what other things would or would not have happened, it was in that neighborhood that we got connected to God's love through Jerry's patience with a family that tried to hide from him.

Here's what happens: You have a story you are writing with your life choices, one moment at time. God desires for his story to intersect with your story and for your story to be changed—for you to realize that you are more than your past and your present circumstances. Between your first day and your final day, there is a much bigger story that you are part of. More importantly, it's not only about you. Your life can have a significant impact on someone else's story!

God wants people to discover his story, and God can use you to help others do exactly that. Think of Paul's words to the curious in Athens: "God who made the world . . . gives all men life and breath and everything else. . . . He determined the times set for them and the exact places where they should live. God did this so that men would seek him and perhaps reach out for him and find him, though he is not far from each one of us" (Acts 17:24-27). As God is involved in orchestrating people's lives—their jobs, their neighborhoods, their life situations—he desires to use you to tell his story so that others will seek and find him. You are an integral link to the connection God desires to have in others' lives.

YOUR LIFE IS A PIECE OF THE PUZZLE

My (Rick's) mother loves to do puzzles. I know I didn't inherit that gene; sitting for hours and agonizing over a small piece of cardboard is not my idea of a good time. Our dining room was home to a puzzle in progress nearly the whole time I was growing up. Occasionally my sister or I sneaked one or two of the puzzle pieces from the table. It was fun to watch Mom go mad when the whole picture was nearly finished and she was missing one or two pieces. The picture was incomplete, and the work wasn't finished. Even though you could tell what the picture was, it was less than satisfying to have a missing piece.

The puzzles Mom had already worked were stored in an upstairs closet between my bedroom and my sister's bedroom until Mom could give them away or sell them at a garage sale. There could be as many as twenty-five puzzles in that closet at one time. One day a friend and I decided that those puzzle pieces would make a great slide. We took twenty to thirty thousand puzzle pieces and filled the hallway floor with them. Then we took turns diving across them. It was a great time until it dawned on me that there was no way to get those puzzle pieces back into the right boxes. Of course, who said they had to go back into the *right* boxes? (I wonder how many of those garage sale shoppers are still trying today to put those puzzles together.)

Sometimes your life may look like an insignificant cardboard piece— not even a border piece or one with an obvious place to fit into. You might even think some of the puzzle pieces in your box belong in other boxes! You wonder what good this life is—not much value, not much significance, nearly useless. But this is God's picture, his puzzle. He knows what he's doing. If the Bible is right, then God indicates that your part of the puzzle is needed, valued, and planned for.

So who are you? What is your life? That all depends. You can simply collect all that has been tossed into your being. You can be defined by your successes and failures or limited by the unfortunate things that have happened to you. *Or* you can be a person who sees your life as on loan from God, to be used, enjoyed, and lived in such a way that God's story is being written through your story—and your story is impacting the stories of others.

WHAT ABOUT YOU?

1. How do you describe who you are?

2. How have the circumstances of your life shaped your story?

3. How do you describe your purpose in life?

4. Who are some people for whom you are grateful, people God has used to impact your story? How did they do so?

2
MORE THAN MEDIOCRE

I have never met anyone who planned on having

a mediocre life, but I have met plenty of mediocre people.

—HOWARD HENDRICKS

ow does it happen that we plan on living exciting lives but end up living mediocre ones? How is it that we settle for less than what we know is possible?

Chris's life was a disaster. He couldn't keep a job or a relationship. Drugs and alcohol consumed his time. There are those who would have liked to describe his life as mediocre—that would have constituted an improvement! Today Chris runs a center in Tulsa, Oklahoma, that helps men and women through their addictions and back onto their feet by providing counseling, mentoring, job training, places to live, and temporary jobs. The hope and dignity he extends to people in Tulsa are far from mediocre.

How did Chris's life change so dramatically? The same way it nearly always happens. Chris met someone, Anna, in a twelve-step group, and she shared her story with him. She explained how God helped her change her story and how her life was now different. Anna chose to invest her story in helping others to connect with God's story—and Chris happened to be at one of those intersections that God had prepared in advance. Chris encountered God's grace at the intersection . . . and now he is finding ways for his story to connect with the stories of others and is introducing them to lives of purpose and meaning. After discovering God through Anna's testimony, Chris started making better choices in his life. And that has made all the difference in changing the direction of his story.

DETOUR AHEAD

The Bible shares the true-life story of Joseph—a man who knew all about dealing with detours. His life had taken plenty of them. At seventeen, Joseph was already reporting on his father's shepherds—his older brothers, in fact. The special privileges given to Joseph by his father, Jacob, caused some extreme jealousy among Joseph's brothers. The Bible says "they hated him" (Genesis 37:4). Maybe you recall the story of Joseph and his beautiful coat, given as a special gift from his father? Joseph not only had a special coat, he also had dreams (though not the ability to interpret those dreams until later). One of his dreams showed his brothers bowing down to him. That dream, combined with the coat, was the straw that broke the camel's back, so to speak.

Joseph's brothers first plotted to kill him but then chose another path. They threw him into a dried-up well, only later to sell him into slavery. Finally, Joseph was taken to Egypt and sold again, this time to a man named Potiphar. In that household, Joseph became a trusted servant, taking care of the affairs of the household. Just when things were beginning to get brighter for Joseph, Potiphar's wife took a liking to him and got him into a heap of trouble by wrongfully accusing Joseph of attempted rape. In that setting, a person was not "innocent until proven guilty." Joseph was simply sent to prison for an undetermined amount of time.

As a favored seventeen-year-old, Joseph certainly didn't foresee or plan any of these things as his ideal future. (Remember, he was dreaming that people bowed before him!) These events (and many more) all seemed like unfair detours in his life. There are three things evident in Joseph's life that helped him deal with the detours.

1) He was a man of integrity. During Joseph's youth, he reported honestly to his father regarding the behavior of the other shepherds. Later, when Joseph was being seduced by Potiphar's wife, he refused her advances. His life was full of injustices, but Joseph never compromised integrity and truth.

2) He never lost sight of his dreams. He was able to see beyond the difficulties. God had given him a vision of what was to come: leadership. He never gave up on the big picture.

3) He trusted God. Regardless of his circumstances, Joseph did not lose his faith. The Bible says, "The LORD was with Joseph and gave him success in whatever he did" (Genesis 39:23). Even while in prison, Joseph was revered, honored, and successful. Eventually, Joseph was reunited with his family. And he was second in command of all Egypt—for close to eighty years. But for thirteen long years Joseph was detoured from his dreams. For the person in the middle of such a detour, every minute seems like a lifetime.

A MIXTURE OF TRASH AND TREASURE

If you were to line up a bunch of trash cans—new, beat up, tall, and short—and sort through the contents of each of them, what would you find? Most likely you would find a lot of trash, and sometimes you would come across a little treasure. Just like Joseph's life, each person's life is a mixture of the good and the bad. Things get put into the "cans" of your life. Some things you choose to put in—education, activities, relationships—and some things are shoved in by others. Some of those things are good, and some are junk (like being thrown into a pit and sold into slavery by your own family). All of it, the trash and the treasure, plays a part in shaping your life, defining your story, and determining who you are.

> *Each person's life is a mixture of the good and the bad.*

It's a basic truth that what goes into the cans is someday going to come out of the cans. Good or bad—the things that get stuffed into the cans *are* going to come out. Sometimes we are good at shoving the stuff down and keeping it manageable. We learn to live around the issues, or with the issues, and sometimes we even pretend the issues don't exist. Look inside the cans—who are you? Are you who you want to be? Are you watching what is coming out? What does it all say about who you are?

When we look at life, most of us generally land in one of two camps.

"I like my life"

One camp says, "My life is good. Oh, occasionally I don't like some things, but I am happy with my life. I can manage the stuff that isn't so good. I'm the master of my own destiny. I am in control."

But what if your life could be better? While you are drifting on the sea of contentment, what if you were created for a greater purpose and have somehow missed that? What if your life could be more fulfilling, more intentional—but because you are sailing along, you missed out on a better adventure? One sage wrote, "If your train is on the wrong track, every station you come to is the wrong station." What if you are on the wrong track?

"I don't like my life"

The second camp says, "I wish I had somebody else's life. I'm not loved, I'm angry, and I am stuck. It isn't fair. I want a different life."

In no way would I discount the things (many of them tragic) that have shaped, marked, or scarred anyone's life. All of our lives are shaped by our own choices and the choices of others. But from God's perspective, we are more than the stuff that has been shoved into the cans. We are more than our past and more than the issues that may haunt us. God has given us life, and what we do with it matters a great deal to him.

If anyone wants a new life, God is thrilled: "Good idea! Let's get you a new life. Let's get rid of some of this trash in your life that keeps messing you up. Some of it we will toss, and some of it we can recycle. You may have to live with a few of the consequences of those things, but they won't have to continue to define your life. I want to do something with your life. I want to renew it, restore it, reconcile it, and rebuild it. I want you to know that your story matters because it is part of a much bigger story that I am writing."

Here's how he says that in the Bible: "It is by grace you have been saved, through faith—and this not from yourselves, it is the gift of God—not by works, so that no one can boast" (Ephesians 2:8, 9). Those words of Paul are significant to living a life on loan. We'll refer to them again in this book. You can't fix life all on your own. You can't change the past, just like I can't change the fact that my grandmother ran away and joined the circus. But through God's grace, your story line can take a different turn. You can have a new identity in him. And once you encounter his grace at the intersections of life, you can start making different choices—not choices that are mediocre but choices that are good, lasting, and noble.

THE NOBLE VS. THE FOOLISH

The dictionary describes *noble* in two ways. First, it is a person of aristocratic line, of high birth, or exalted rank. Second, it defines a person possessing outstanding qualities. It is obviously this second meaning of *noble* that Isaiah had in mind when he said, "The noble man makes noble plans, and by noble deeds he stands" (Isaiah 32:8). In the earlier verses of chapter 32, Isaiah describes the fool in contrast to the noble man.

> No longer will the fool be called noble, or the rogue be spoken of as generous. For a fool speaks nonsense, and his heart inclines toward wickedness, to practice ungodliness and to speak error against the LORD, to keep the hungry person unsatisfied and to withhold drink from the thirsty. As for a rogue, his weapons are evil; he devises wicked schemes to destroy the afflicted with slander, even though the needy one speaks what is right (vv. 5-7, *NASB*).

Fools lack generosity, speak nonsense, are ungodly, do not speak the truth, and see needs but ignore them. Fools live their lives focused on themselves. The Bible describes the fool as selfish (not stupid)—self-serving, self-seeking, and self-centered. This is how *not* to be noble.

The fool withholds from those in need

Over and over throughout the Bible, God invites us to find ways to help—to use our resources not simply for meeting our own needs but to help meet the needs of others. All of us know people who are generous—they give and find joy in helping others. A generous person doesn't have to be wealthy—but he does need a big heart.

We are bombarded daily with the message that life is about us, our needs, our desires, and that we are entitled to whatever we want. Marketing ads are designed to convince us that we won't be happy until we buy what they are selling. In some way, shape, or form, you have probably bought into that message. You might give to a special need or give to save some taxes, but are you really generous? Do you find ways to be generous—to intentionally meet the needs of another individual with no expectation of a return?

To commemorate a special occasion, Ken's grandson gave him a very nice pocket watch. Engraved on the back of the watch were the words "To the man who taught me to be generous." Ken exemplifies the noble person. If you knew Ken, you might describe him as a shrewd businessman or tough boss, but for those who really know him, *generous* is the only appropriate description. He is generous with his money, his things, and his time. He chooses to give when there is a need— without fanfare and without regard for

A generous person doesn't have to be wealthy—but he does need a big heart.

how others might be giving. He regularly asks, "Is there something that I can help with?" His quiet but influential generosity has been a blessing to many and a lesson for those close to him.

The fool practices ungodliness and speaks error

Isaiah's words about the fool don't tell us whether the fool knows the truth and ignores it or has never discovered the truth. What Isaiah does say is that the fool will say or be whatever he needs to say or be to get his way—even if it means somehow speaking falsely about God. Of course, God can take care of his own reputation, but the fool seems willing to tamper with it to get what he wants.

Isaiah doesn't describe the choices fools make that put them in the position of being called ungodly, but we know that becoming ungodly is about choice. The fool makes choices that eventually take him away from God. You and I are capable of doing the same thing. More often than not, our foolish choices lead us to that place away from God by one small choice at a time. The poet Carl Sandburg said, "There is an eagle in me that wants to soar, and there is a hippopotamus in me that wants to wallow in the mud."[1] It is the hippo that gets me into trouble, that tries to keep me wallowing in ungodliness.

How can you avoid foolish choices? God's invitation is to know the truth revealed in the Bible. Are you content with never reading the Bible or never letting someone else read it to you or tell you about it? Declining God's invitation to read his Word results in a life lived by error and half-truths.

Half-truths are the things that, on the surface, sound as if they'd make life better. Believing half-truths allows us to live with our inconsistencies, justify our behavior, and manage our way (sort of) through the chaos. There are thousands of these half-truths. Here are just a couple of them:

- "I know I shouldn't get so angry, but it is the only way things get done around here."
- "So I drink a little. Sometimes the little becomes a lot, but it's the only way I can relax when I get stressed out."

A common example of living with half-truths occurs at the kids' bedtime. Dad asks his kids to head to bed, but no one moves. Dad waits a bit and then yells louder. Finally, Dad gets up and yells and screams, and then the kids jump up and go to bed. The half-truth Dad believes is that the only way to get the kids to respond is to yell and scream.

Half-truths are insidious and keep people behaving in ways they think work—like bosses bullying employees to get things done, spouses pouting so the other spouse gives in, or children crying to get their way. Often these half-truths are so ingrained that we are convinced beyond a shadow of a doubt that they are true and that's the way life works or, at least, "This is true for me."

Do you live, act, or behave in accordance with half-truths? Sometimes the half-truth causes pain in your life, but you live with it because you don't know any other way. Half-truths may seem to work for a while, but one day you'll find they don't work for you like they used to. You won't be able to yell loud enough or pout long enough to make things work. These half-truths will no longer fix your problems, relieve your pain, stop your chaos, or bring light into darkness.

God offers his *whole* truth. "You will know the truth, and the truth will set you free" (John 8:32). What will God's truth free you from? From error . . . from all of those half-truths that clutter up your life and cause you to live in chaos.

> *God's truth will give you an anchoring point and a compass for living.*

Truth is a hard thing to discuss today. We live in a time when truth is whatever we need it to be. Truth has been reduced to whatever makes us feel good or justifies our actions. Even followers of God play with his truth. There was a bumper sticker that was popular among Christians for a while: "God said it, I believe it, and that settles it." That sounds good—makes for a nice bumper sticker. However, it makes a subtle but significant change in God's truth. *God said it*—he has spoken. *I believe it*—the veracity rises or falls based on my believing it. *That settles it*—it is done. In other words, God and I have decided what is true. That bumper sticker should read: "God said it and that settles it, whether I believe it or not."

Have you pursued truth? I am convinced that God's truth will give you an anchoring point and a compass for living. The noble person will be involved in discovering the whole truth of God and learning to live with that truth. Honestly, it isn't always easy. You may not like some of the things God has to say, and you will sometimes desire to make different choices. God's invitation is to discover his truth and see what that truth does in and through your life.

The fool leaves the hungry and thirsty wanting

Even basic human needs go unmet by the fool. It is within his ability, his resources, and his opportunities to share food and water—the basics. Yet the hungry go to sleep unsatisfied, and the thirsty are left craving. In your self-absorbed moments, do you assume that anyone who wishes can have his basic needs taken care of? Do you think that people who are hungry and thirsty are somehow just lazy or less worthy than you? The truth is that even in the midst of great opportunity and wealth, there are those who are unable to provide even their own most basic needs.

But the noble person is involved in meeting these needs.

In June 2002, Dallas, a high-level business executive, heard God's call to go out and serve the homeless population of Virginia Beach, Virginia.[2] He wasn't trying to start a ministry. He felt he was only being obedient to God. Over the next six months, the people Dallas and his family were serving grew from five to about sixty. "It became too much for just my family so God called others to come help us," he shares. In May 2004, this band of simply obedient people became a nonprofit ministry called PIN (People In Need). PIN now serves over two hundred homeless people in Norfolk and Virginia Beach, Virginia, every Sunday and has over thirty dedicated volunteers. They provide food, hygiene supplies, clothing, and medical care. "My wife and I have decided that this is what God wants us to do for the rest of our lives, so we sold our house and bought a house half the size." Dallas has enrolled at Regent University to work on a divinity degree. He doesn't feel that he was called to become a pastor, but he realized that God has called him to more than making sandwiches and business deals.

One day Dallas was at a Wendy's restaurant helping one homeless person when another lady who had been helped by PIN came running in. She needed five more dollars to have enough money for a hotel room. Dallas realized she hadn't eaten for a while, so he bought her dinner. After they ate, they walked over to the hotel. The lady said to the clerk, "My pastor is here to pay the difference for my hotel room." Dallas isn't sure whether she had ever been to church or not, and he wasn't sure he was called to be a pastor. "But I *was* her pastor," shares Dallas. In Matthew 25:40 Jesus said that what you do for the needy, you do for him. Dallas felt good getting Jesus a hotel room that night!

In June 2002 when Dallas's family heard God's invitation to serve, they didn't know where it would take them. They simply obeyed. God has blessed their ministry of providing for those who are hungry and thirsty. He's allowed them to be involved with people, whether it's helping them make decisions to accept Jesus Christ, find permanent housing, or simply get a burger at Wendy's.

MAKING NOBLE CHOICES

Truly noble people may seem to be a rare breed, but they are out there (and, hopefully, multiplying). They often go unnoticed, and they rarely make it onto any official list of nobility—but God sees the noble men and women who use their moments to make a difference in someone else's life, even when no one else notices.

An NBA sportscaster was describing the start of the all-star game in Denver: "All the noble players are in town." Today, the people considered noble are the strong, rich, successful, and powerful. There are thousands who, by the world's standards, could be labeled noble. One such person was Princess Diana who was (and is still) adored by millions. Officially, she could carry the noble title. Her marriage to

Prince Charles joined her to the royal family of England. It was the stuff fairy tales are made of—at least in the beginning. She had a kingdom, a crown, and a title. She possessed beauty and charm. More than that, she had power and influence. She could speak a word and it was done or give a command and it was followed. In every sense of the word, by today's standards she was noble. Princess Diana did many good things with her position, her winsome personality, and her highly visible life. Her death was tragic.

It is ironic that within a few days of Princess Diana's death, Mother Teresa also died. Maybe that was God's way of saying, "You want to see noble? I'll show you noble." Mother Teresa didn't have any of the qualities considered noble today. She was poor, not particularly attractive, meek, and humble. She didn't have servants and certainly possessed no crown. Yet this diminutive nun—living among the poorest of the poor and outcast—had power that some only dream of. If Isaiah is right, then God certainly would have declared Mother Teresa among that rare breed of noble people.

You might be thinking, *I can't be like Mother Teresa! I can't influence millions like that. I can't move to the other side of the world and give my remaining days to serving the poor.* Well, maybe you could. Or that may not be what God has called you to do; that may not be the passion he has given you. He might want you to allow his story to change your story and for your story to reach out to touch others right where you are. Mother Teresa's life touched millions because she was first willing to touch one.

Benjamin Franklin wrote, "The noblest question in the world is: What good may I do in it?"[3] It is said that at the beginning of each day he asked himself, "What can I do?" At the end of the day he asked, "Did I do it?"

When you look in the mirror and review your actions and attitudes from this week, what do you see—a foolish person or a noble person? Have most of your actions and words been about helping yourself, maneuvering choices for your gain, or taking care of your own needs? Have you been a fool? Or have you made noble plans?

The noble make noble plans

What are the plans you have? What dreams do you have about your life? If you had the choice, what would you like to have inscribed on your gravestone someday? Surely you wouldn't want it to be: I Didn't Know—I Thought This Was Intermission. I would like mine to read: To Be Continued. Or maybe: A Life on Loan—Well Done!

Are you living based on what really matters most to you? Are you living in a way that will accomplish what you are after? There is an old Chinese proverb that says, "If we keep heading in the same direction, we are likely to get where we are headed." Do you like the direction you are headed? If you don't like the direction you are going and where it is taking you, why keep on going that way?

If you don't like the direction you are going and where it is taking you, why keep on going that way?

The noble person makes noble plans. Do your dreams and plans include God, or are they only about your wants, needs, and future accomplishments? The Bible says, "In his heart a man plans his course, but the LORD determines his steps" (Proverbs 16:9). You have been created with the freedom to choose and the ability to plan and dream. God has given you the aptitude to look for opportunities, to counsel with others, and to determine a path for your life.

I (Rick) will admit there have been plenty of times, maybe too many, when I have been content to do this all by myself—to be the captain of my boat. I haven't invited others to provide advice or guidance and certainly haven't included God in the process. Just as I have been guilty of keeping God out, I also have been guilty of sitting on a rock and waiting for God to send me a detailed set of plans. It's almost as if I have been waiting for a postcard from Heaven telling me which door to choose.

The most peaceful and fulfilling times are when you are on target with both halves of Proverbs 16:9. You need to plan, dream, counsel, and search. You also need to let God determine the steps—as you pray, read Scripture, and ask godly people for their insight.

When I graduated from college, I wasn't really sure I wanted to be in ministry. (I'm still not sure some days!) But I decided that if I did, I wanted to go back to upstate New York to do it. As hard as I tried to make that happen, it simply didn't come together. I didn't want to live in the South or be an associate minister of a church. But through an unusual set of circumstances, I found myself living in Florida and working as an associate minister. Just about the time my wife and I thought we could live there forever, we ended up moving to Cincinnati to work for a college. I didn't really want to do that and thought we would be there only one year. Five years later, while on a trip to Colorado for some meetings, I was invited to fill in for a church that was between ministers. I was thirty-one at the time, our family was young, and we had no interest in the West. I was wrestling with what the next step should be, even with whether or not to stay in occupational ministry. In just a short period of time, we were in a moving truck, relocating our young family to Longmont, Colorado. We have lived there ever since.

Each of those places—although none of them was in my plans—ended up being a source of great experiences and growth for us. In hindsight, I can see God's hand at work in each of those moves—even though I was praying that God would do something different. Lately I have been praying, "Lord, I don't want to move to Hawaii; please don't *ever* send me *there!*"

When you make noble plans, invite God into the journey, and begin to take steps, God can use that to be part of his bigger story. Standing still and waiting for a road map may work for some people, but it has never been how God has guided my life. It's much easier to change the direction of the car when it is moving and headed somewhere than when it is parked in the driveway.

What is it that you dream of? What kind of bold or noble plans are you making? How can God use your story as part of his bigger story?

Thirty-three-year-old truck driver Larry Walters accomplished his dream of flying, even if his aircraft was unconventional. Supposedly, Larry had spent a good deal of his life dreaming of flying but had never had the opportunity until July 2, 1982, when he and several buddies got together. They took an aluminum lawn chair—the kind with those green and white straps—and attached thirty weather balloons to it. Reports vary, but Larry seat-belted himself into the chair and took some peanut butter and jelly sandwiches, a six-pack of beer, a CB radio to report to his friends what he was seeing, and a BB gun to shoot the balloons when he wanted to descend.

The combination of guys, beer, thirty weather balloons, a BB gun, and an aluminum chair are probably what got Larry nominated for the Darwin Awards that year.[4] Instead of leisurely floating over his southern California neighborhood, Larry's chair, when cut loose from its tethers, shot more than two miles into the air—right through the approach corridor to the Long Beach International Airport. Can you imagine airline pilots trying to figure out what in the world they had just seen? Larry started firing his BB gun as fast as he could. When he landed, the police, emergency workers, and a few reporters caught up with him. Larry admitted being scared to death. Reporters asked whether he would ever try this again. "Not in a million years!" he replied. Finally they asked him why he did it. I loved his answer, "You can't just sit there, can you?"[5]

We need more people with that kind of attitude . . . well, maybe without the beer and BB gun. So don't just sit there. There are plenty of noble things to do. There are plenty of opportunities and ways to serve others. There are simple ways for you to be engaged, to get beyond yourself and meet the needs of another. Helping others doesn't have to be dramatic or extravagant. It doesn't mean you have to travel halfway around the world. It *does* mean that you have to make an intentional choice to get involved.

Your experiences, abilities, ideas, and relationships can be the very things that others need for their stories to be impacted when your lives intersect. While there may be heartaches and disappointments, wrong turns and screwups, none of that is wasted with God. Your life story, to this point, can be utilized somehow to make a difference for someone else.

By noble deeds they stand

The noble person doesn't just spend time reading about nobility, learning noble ways, or dreaming about what he or she might end up doing someday. The world is full of those kinds of people. No, the noble person *does* something, gets his hands dirty, finds a way to use what he has, and seizes the opportunities that come.

A number of years ago, I began praying a very simple prayer every morning as my feet hit the floor: "God, all day long today I am going to have the opportunity to choose. Help me to choose well. Help me to choose you." I wish I could say that I live that prayer out all day long every day, but I don't. Sometimes I am self-centered and make poor choices. With big choices, it seems easier for me to be intentional, focused, and more conscientious about doing the right thing. But most of my everyday life is full of little choices. Unfortunately, bad little choices can pile up until they constitute the bulk of a lifetime—crowding out the good bigger choices that could have been made.

If someone were to give you $525,600, what would you do with it? Don't spend a ton of energy thinking about it, because it's not likely to happen. You might choose to pay off some debts, buy a new home, take an exotic vacation, help some family members or friends, give to a church, invest in stocks or real estate, save, or spend it all. You might choose to consult with a financial adviser who would help you develop a plan. There are lots and lots of ways you could use that money.

The only moment you and I have is this one. You can't get back the moments you have spent, and there's no guarantee of the moments ahead.

This year you'll have 525,600 minutes. What are you doing with them? What kind of investment are you making with your life? In reality, at the end of the day, your life is simply a piling up of all your moments, isn't it? There might be some really big moments in the mix of that pile, but most are pretty ordinary and seemingly in-significant. Yet it is the moment-by-moment choices that make a life.

I always carry an emergency hundred-dollar bill in my wallet. It is a rare occasion when I have to use it, but one day I was out of cash and was at a place that didn't take credit cards. I had to break my hundred-dollar bill to pay for an eight-dollar meal. I had been carrying that particular hundred-dollar bill for at least three months. It's funny how it took me only two days to spend the remaining ninety-two dollars. Once that one hundred dollars was broken into smaller amounts, it slipped right through my hands. I couldn't even tell you where it went. If I had a million dollars, I would pay more attention to it (I think!). I would want to make wise choices with it. But one hundred dollars seems like no big deal and is much easier to treat more casually.

The little things *are* a big deal. The only moment you and I have is this one. You can't get back the moments you have spent, and there's no guarantee of the moments ahead. You get to spend your life one moment at a time in lots of little choices. A noble person uses the moments to make noble plans and to do noble deeds. What an excellent foundation on which to stand!

Noble deeds start at home

Love is the basis for noble deeds. Our love for others outside our homes means little if we don't first start by loving those *in* our homes. How we practically express love for our families is where the rubber meets the road. Like all other relationships, family relationships are gifts on loan from God.

Scott is a good friend and very successful businessman. He has the ability to zero in on what is most important. One day Scott was reviewing a conversation he'd had with a neighbor who was having family difficulties. Just as Jesus was able to reduce the entire Old Testament to the irreducible minimum of loving God and loving others (see Matthew 22:37-39), Scott (though far from being a theologian) articulated very simply what he had discovered about love within family relationships. "I've found there are really only four things the Bible says about families," he said. "Children are to honor their parents (Exodus 20:12), fathers are not to exasperate their children (Ephesians 6:4), husbands are to love their wives (Ephesians 5:28), and wives are to respect their husbands (Ephesians 5:33)." We like his approach.

Honor your parents

Jesus himself provides a good example of what it means to honor one's parents throughout the different stages of life. When Jesus was twelve years old, he joined a discussion with the wisest teachers in Jerusalem.

When Mary and Joseph found him, the Scriptures say, "he went down to Nazareth with them and was obedient to them" (Luke 2:51). Obedience is an appropriate way for children to honor parents.

When Jesus grew into adulthood, he honored his mother by treating her as an honored peer (see John 2:1-8). (There is a conspicuous absence of Jesus' earthly father, Joseph, who presumably had died.) As adults we don't honor our parents through obedience but through assuming adult responsibility for our lives. We best honor our parents by living in a way that says "I have the values I need to live on my own, make my own decisions, and take responsibility before God and society for my choices." After we become adults, our parents are there to counsel us but not to be obeyed.

As our parents age, we express our love by caring for them or seeing that they are cared for. In many ways the roles of parent and child are often reversed as children of aging parents become caregivers. First Timothy 5:4 says we "should learn first of all to put [our] religion into practice by caring for [our] own family and so repaying [our] parents and grandparents, for this is pleasing to God." When Jesus was on the cross, he loved and honored his mother by seeing to it that she would be cared for after he was gone (John 19:26, 27).

What every child needs

Psalm 127:3 (*NLT*) says, "Children are a gift from the LORD"—on loan from God while we have them with us. Children need to be told frequently that we love them, that we are glad to be a family with them, and that we affirm who they are and who they are becoming. While Jesus was coming out of the water after being baptized, his Father spoke audibly to him and said, "You are my Son, whom I love; with you I am well pleased" (Mark 1:11). These few words express what every child longs to hear from a father.

1) Belonging and attachment—"You are my son." If you've ever observed a crawling baby leave the presence of a parent to venture into another room, you know he or she soon returns just to be certain the parent is still there. The parent's presence creates security and a sense of belonging. Without a sense of belonging, children often grow up without the ability to emotionally bond with others. When you say to your child "You belong to me," you are creating an emotional bond of love. Frequently tell your children how proud you are to be their mom or dad and how happy you are to be with them.

2) Unconditional love—"Whom I love." Every child on earth longs to be loved unconditionally. I (Eric) once overheard a young mother tell her preschool daughter, "Mommy doesn't love you when you are bad." That type of statement communicates conditional worth and conditional acceptance—that love is something to be earned. Real love is without condition. Kids will test the conditions of your love, but you need to let them know that they can never do anything that will stop you from loving them. God's love was expressed verbally. It is not enough to feel love. Lavishly tell your kids that you love them as God loved his Son.

3) Affirmation and approval—"With you I am well pleased." Every child longs to have the admiration and approval of his mom and dad. This is admiration, approval, and affirmation for who a child is—not for what he or she does. Your being "well pleased" communicates to the children that they have intrinsic worth and value. The timing of the Father's words to Jesus is interesting. He was well pleased with Jesus *before* Jesus called his disciples, performed his first miracle, or fulfilled his earthly mission. The Father was well pleased with Jesus simply because he was who he was.

Love your wives

Several times throughout the Scriptures, husbands are commanded to love their wives. Love, the verb, is different than love, the emotion. If we wait to willfully love until we feel the emotions of love, we may be waiting a long time. Love, the emotion, is often the fruit of love, the verb. In Ephesians 5, the apostle Paul uses three different comparisons to help husbands know how to love their wives. He probably figured out that most men are too thickheaded to get it with just one comparison.

First he writes, "Husbands, love your wives, just as Christ loved the church and gave himself up for her" (v. 25). Most men can weasel out of this one by muttering something like "Well, I'm not perfect like Jesus, so that gets me off the hook." So Paul takes another stab at it when he says, "Husbands ought to love their wives as their own bodies" (v. 28). Now he's getting a bit closer to home. But if one still doesn't understand, Paul continues, "He who loves his wife loves himself. After all, no one ever hated his own body, but he feeds and cares for it" (vv. 28, 29). Now we get that one. Taking care of ourselves is not dependent on how we feel about ourselves at the moment. John Gray, author of *Men Are from Mars, Women Are from Venus*, captures this idea.

> When a man is in love, he begins to care about another as much as himself. He is suddenly released from the binding chains of being motivated for himself alone and becomes free to give to another, not for personal gain, but out of caring. He experiences his partner's fulfillment as if it were his own. He can easily endure any hardship to make her happy because her happiness makes him happy. His struggles become easier. He is energized with a higher purpose.[6]

In Ecclesiastes 9:9 God says to husbands, "Enjoy life with your wife, whom you love, all the days of this . . . life that God has given you under the sun." Living a life that pleases God involves loving your wife. How do we love our wives? By loving them as Christ loved the church, as we love our own bodies, and as we love ourselves.

Respect your husbands

The speaker at a women's conference queried the audience: "How many of you want to mother your husbands?" A single hand timidly raised above the crowd. "What!? You want to mother your husband?" the speaker asked incredulously. The woman with the raised hand answered with chagrin, "Mother? Oh, I thought you said smother."

Men want to be neither mothered nor smothered by their wives. In the Bible, women are not commanded to love their husbands but to respect them (Ephesians 5:33). In the book *For Women Only—What You Need to Know About the Inner Lives of Men*, author Shaunti Feldhahn reports that she surveyed more than one thousand men and notes that "home is the most important place for a man to be affirmed. If a man knows that his wife believes in him, he is empowered to do better in every area of his life. A man tends to think of life as a competition and a battle, and he can energetically go duke it out if he can come home to someone who supports him unconditionally, who will wipe his brow and tell him he can do it."[7] What men want most from women is respect—to see that the women have confidence that the men can slay the dragons.

Every relationship of love is on loan from God. We don't want to control the people in our relationships, but we can nurture the relationships and watch them grow.

THE 1–1–1 PRINCIPLE

What are some practical ways to instill in your life the values of a noble person—both at home and at the intersections of your life? Consider the 1–1–1 approach: one hour of worship, one hour of personal growth, and one hour of service. That amounts to only three hours a week. When you think about the fact that there are one hundred sixty-eight hours in each week, three hours doesn't sound like much. But since we rush, run, squeeze, and manage, trying to maximize our time, three hours could be a lot. In any event, these three hours will be multiplied and magnified if we are willing to invest them.

One hour of worship

Worship is critical. Through worship God is honored, and we are challenged and are given the opportunity to connect with others and grow in our relationship with God. Sometimes we allow things to get in the way of worship. Plenty of activities call for our attention and sometimes pull us away from that one hour of worship. Make worship a priority for you personally and for your family. Commit to attending the worship service at a local church. Most

Make worship a priority for you personally and for your family.

churches work hard at creating services that honor God. However, worship isn't just about what you can gain; it is also about what you can give to the community of faith.

One hour of personal growth

While worship provides an opportunity to gather with others and honor God, we also need to grow in our faith. That is hour number two. Find a place to grow personally. Spend that hour of study in a small group, a home Bible study, a class, or some self-study opportunity. Growing spiritually is a biblical challenge and a personal responsibility. If you will take the time to look, you will find an option for study that will enrich and grow your faith. The Bible is a gift just waiting for you to open it.

One hour of service

One hour of serving others each week doesn't seem like much, until you consider that the average American serves less than five hours a year. God is honored when we serve him. At LifeBridge Christian Church, we tell our members that whether their service is in our church or in the community, it doesn't matter to us. If you are serving to benefit others and to honor God, then you will be blessed. And often it is by serving others that you earn the right to share your story.

The 1–1–1 principle. Three hours out of one hundred sixty-eight. It is only 2 percent of your week, but God can use that 2 percent of your time in a grand way. Those three hours have the potential to be multiplied and become a great blessing in your life. Who knows how God might use those three hours to make a kingdom difference? You may have to give up some things to commit three hours to these new things. But consider these words from *Inc.* magazine: "While pleasures . . . bring fleeting happiness that lessens in intensity over time, . . . gratification is a longer-lasting joy that requires skill and effort and can only be had by activity consonant with noble purpose. . . . To achieve happiness you must enjoy doing your best while contributing to something beyond yourself."[8]

Make noble plans, stand by noble deeds, and your life will move beyond mediocrity and into moments of significance for God.

WHAT ABOUT YOU?

1. What causes you to settle for mediocrity in your life?

2. What are some good things that have come out of the detours you have had to take?

3. What are the half-truths you choose to live with?

4. What is the whole truth of God you need to apply in your life?

5. How can you be reminded of God's love for you at this moment?

6. What noble plan could you implement this week at home or in your community?

3

SAVED *FROM* SOMETHING *FOR* SOMETHING

My faith demands—this is not optional—

my faith demands that I do whatever I can, wherever I am,

whenever I can, for as long as I can with

whatever I have to try to make a difference.

—JIMMY CARTER

n 1981, I (Eric) was recruited to help get the word out and sell tickets for an unknown film called *Chariots of Fire*. I was given several ten-packs of tickets and asked to sell them to folks in my Christian circles or give them to my neighbors. Much to everyone's surprise, the film eventually captured the attention of the nation and the Motion Picture Academy by winning Best Picture of 1981. The story line highlights two athletes preparing for and then competing in the 1924 Olympic Games in Paris. One of the featured athletes in the film is Scotland's Eric Liddell, who is dubbed the Flying Scotsman. In the film, as Liddell is competing in the finals of the 200-meter race, he pulls away from the pack and with his head tilted back and a smile on his face, we hear his thoughts in a voice-over: "God made me for a purpose, but he also made me fast. And when I run I feel his pleasure." This is the affirmation of someone who has found his calling. Liddell was a committed Christian who went on to serve God as a missionary in China after the games were completed.

Are there times when you feel God's pleasure in what you're doing? Have you discovered the place where your passion intersects with God's purpose and you feel fully alive? A life on loan is filled with purpose and passion. This isn't an accident. God has created each person with a purpose in mind. One of the all-time best-selling books is Rick Warren's *The Purpose-Driven Life.* It is a profound and powerful book that has sold tens of millions of copies, been translated into dozens of languages, and been embraced even by people who don't normally read Christian books. The subtitle of the book is *What On Earth Am I Here For?* No book on discovering God-given purpose has captured the attention of our world like this book. It's obvious that people sense they are here to do *something*; they're just not sure what that something is.

> *Each of us is created and designed by God to do something that he prepared beforehand for us to do.*

For the past forty years, the Higher Education Research Institute at UCLA has been conducting a comprehensive survey on the attitudes and values of incoming freshmen. The 2004 study was based on the responses of more than one hundred twelve thousand freshmen at 236 colleges and universities. According to this study, "79% say they believe in God, 69% say they pray, and 76% say they are searching for purpose or meaning."[1] Helen Astin, co-principal investigator of the study, observes, "They are searching for answers to big questions: What is the meaning of life? What is my purpose in life? What will happen to me? Will I leave my mark in this world?"[2]

Discovering purpose is not a longing just of college students but of every human heart. God delights in revealing his purpose to us. Each of us is created and designed by God to do something that he prepared beforehand for us to do. He designed us not only to *be* someone but also to *do* something! Brennan Manning captured this idea when he said, "When being is divorced from doing, pious thoughts become a substitute for washing dirty feet."[3]

As we read the Scriptures, we discover that the Bible is full of verses that both relate to finding purpose and give directions on how to find it.

- God gives us leaders to *prepare us* for good works: "It was he who gave some to be apostles, some to be prophets, some to be evangelists, and some to be pastors and teachers, to prepare God's people for works of service, so that the body of Christ may be built up" (Ephesians 4:11, 12).

- God gives us the Bible to *equip us* for good works: "All Scripture is God-breathed and is useful for teaching, rebuking, correcting and training in righteousness, so that the man of God may be thoroughly equipped for every good work" (2 Timothy 3:16, 17).

- God gives us spiritual gifts to *enable us* to do good works: "Each one should use whatever gift he has received to serve others, faithfully administering God's grace in its various forms" (1 Peter 4:10).

- God gives us other Christians to *spur us on* toward good works: "Let us consider how we may spur one another on toward love and good deeds" (Hebrews 10:24).

Think about this. You are created in Christ Jesus to do good works. God gives you leaders to prepare you for those good works, the Bible to equip you for those good works, spiritual gifts to enable you to do good works, and others to encourage you to do good works. Do you think he's trying to tell you something?

TWO QUESTIONS

These two aspects of our lives of faith (who we are and what we do) have lasting implications. One day we will stand before God to "give an account" (Romans 14:12) of ourselves. The way I see it, we each will have two questions to answer. The first question will be something like "Why should I let you into Heaven?" And the correct answer to that question is "I am trusting Jesus Christ alone for my salvation (see Ephesians 2:8, 9). He said if I believed in him I would not die but have everlasting life" (John 3:16).

But there is also a second question. Paul writes, "We make it our goal to please him, whether we are at home in the body or away from it. For we must all appear before the judgment seat of Christ, that each one may receive what is due him for the things done while in the body, whether good or bad" (2 Corinthians 5:9, 10). The second question centers on what you did here on earth. It might be something like "What did you do to love, help, and serve others?"

You'll have to give an account for what you did for others as a result of knowing Christ. What did you do for the hungry, the thirsty, the strangers, the sick, and the prisoners (see Matthew 25:31-46)?

You can't answer the second question with the answer to the first question any more than you can answer the first question with the answer to the second question. If that sounded a bit like double-talk, here's some clarification. When God asks you why he should let you into Heaven, your correct answer is not "Because of all of the good things I've done."

Remember that salvation is a gift from God. You can't earn it. Likewise, when God asks "What did you do for others?" your answer can't be "When I was a teenager, I walked down the aisle in church and accepted Christ as my Savior." That's the type of answer that serves you well for the first question but not for the second. The right answer for the second question is to tell God how you used the life that he loaned you—what you did to help, love, and serve others that connected them to God's grace. God wants to hear about how you loved your neighbors as yourself as an extension of his love to you.

The two-question concept stems from what is called the Great Commandment, found in Matthew 22:37-39. When Jesus was asked what the greatest commandment in all of Scripture was, his answer was twofold—in short, to love God and to love people. It makes sense that he will ask you, "Well . . . how did you do in loving me and loving others?"

When we live a life on loan, we really have the questions answered ahead of time. We belong to him. That answers the first question. Our passion for God should then automatically motivate us to right actions. That answers the second question.

TWO VACUUMS

Your life has a God-shaped vacuum

In the seventeenth century, French philosopher, mathematician, and physicist Blaise Pascal penned these words, "There is a God shaped vacuum in the heart of every man which cannot be filled by any created thing, but only by God, the Creator, made known through Jesus."[4]

He was right. As a physicist he knew something about vacuums. But it doesn't take a scientist to know what a vacuum feels like. Several centuries earlier Aurelius Augustinus, later to be known as Saint Augustine, wrote of God in his *Confessions,* "You have made us and directed us toward yourself and our heart is restless until we rest in you."[5] God has created a place in your heart for himself, and you will always feel a sense of incompleteness or emptiness until he takes his rightful place. No accomplishment, achievement, fortune, or fame can fill that void. He created a space that he alone can dwell in. When you receive God's gift of salvation, that vacuum is filled.

> *God has created a place in your heart for himself, and you will always feel a sense of incompleteness or emptiness until he takes his rightful place.*

A story is told about a man who died and went to Heaven, where he saw a sign hanging on the pearly gates that read: "To enter you must have one hundred points." The man was then asked by Saint Peter, "Why should I let you into Heaven?"

The recently deceased and eulogized man gave a litany of reasons why he should be allowed into Heaven. "Well . . . I've been a good man . . . I tried to do the right thing. Let's see . . . I was a deacon in my church for seven years . . . uh, I went on a mission trip to Mexico where I painted a cinder-block church and ate bad food. Um, I've been a faithful husband and good father and tried to love my neighbor as myself. How's that? How many points did I get?"

Saint Peter answered, "Well . . . let's see now . . . add three . . . carry the two . . . time off for good behavior . . . The final total is zero points."

"Zero points?!" the man exclaimed. "You mean all the good I did adds up to zero? If that's true, it's only by the grace of God that I'll get into this place!"

"Now that's one hundred points. Come on in."

That's what grace does. Christ comes into your life apart from any personal works you could ever boast about. Salvation can't be earned or merited. It comes as God's gift to us. God, and God alone, fills the God-shaped vacuum.

Your life has a purpose-shaped vacuum

There is another vacuum in each life that is just as real. Ephesians 2:10 states that you "are God's workmanship, created in Christ Jesus to do good works, which God prepared in advance for us to do." In other words, you've been given this life because God has something for you to do. He's already planned and prepared how your story can be part of the bigger story. God, who has repaired your soul, also extends his grace to fix the hole in your heart—the purpose-shaped vacuum.

Your life matters. It counts. You can—and do—make a difference in the world. But for most of us, it's easy to feel fairly insignificant and not of much value. All of us, if we are honest, have moments when we wonder whether our lives really matter or what difference we can possibly make. This reflects the purpose-shaped vacuum. The verse says, "We are God's workmanship." That is, he created us exactly according to his specs and design. And he's also created each person "to do good works, which [he] prepared in advance for us to do." Because God has prepared these good works in advance, that creates a vacuum for you—not to invent but to discover and step into.

Unlike the God-shaped vacuum that's one size fits all, the purpose-shaped vacuum is individual. Yours is found at the intersection of the way he has made you and what he wants to accomplish in this world through you. So think of all God cares about in this world . . . all that is on his agenda. God has designed you with a predisposed passion to co-labor with him in doing what he wants done. Wow, that's a pretty huge responsibility—but God thinks you're up for it!

God's hope, his plan, is for you to know his love. His invitation is for you to discover his grace, grow in that grace, and learn to extend that grace. When you allow God's grace to show up in your life, you can live passionately for him. Your purpose-shaped vacuum will be filled. And the grace you know will spill over into other people's lives.

Most pastors, missionaries, and other vocational Christian workers will say that they frequently experience the intersection of their passions with God's purpose, where they feel God's pleasure. And some people believe that this intersection is reserved *only* for those who are in the full-time Christian service professions. But it can and should be the normal experience for every believer—including you. The second vacuum is filled when you spend your time passionately doing what God has given you to do.

A TWO-PART STORY

Do you have a story that tells about how you met Christ and the difference he has made in your life? Most Christians do. Normally this story, or testimony, centers on the enrichment in your life since Christ entered it—because you have Jesus, you have more peace, more joy, and less worry. You may describe some of those improvements this way: "I used to lose my temper, but now I'm more patient" or "I used to drink all the time, but now I only drink when I'm depressed, celebrating something, or with my friends."

But that's really only one aspect of your story, isn't it? That part centers on what God saved you *from*. But the second piece should be all about what God saved you *for*. This is the portion you share with others about how knowing Christ can help make this world a better place. Wouldn't the world be different if all Christians had the second component to accompany the first?

On December 26, 2004, a giant tsunami rolled over the coastlines of South Asia, taking its tragic toll in property and tens of thousands of human lives. Countless people were left homeless and orphaned. On January 7, 2005, TV host Larry King (at the suggestion of former president Bill Clinton) invited representatives of different faiths to come on the *Larry King Live* show to express their views regarding faith in a loving God during a time of tragedy.[6] On the panel were R. Albert Mohler Jr., president of the Southern Baptist Theological Seminary; Deepak Chopra, New Age spiritual adviser; Michael Manning, a Roman Catholic priest; Dr. Maher Hathout, Muslim scholar and retired physician; Michael Lerner, a rabbi; and Henepola Gunaratana, one of the senior monks at the Buddhist Vihara Temple in Queens, New York. Each one of them was asked, "How do we find God after losing so much in a historic tragedy? How much is our faith in a higher power tested by the tsunami killing more than 150,000 people in a matter of moments?" Despite the mental and spiritual acumen represented, it was hard to find a satisfying answer.

Perhaps the best apologetic, or answer, to this question is a combination of healthy agnosticism coupled with rock-hard certainty: "You know, I could give you some classic answers regarding what philosophers and theologians have written throughout the ages, but to be honest, I really haven't a clue. What I do know with absolute and crystal-clear certainty is how Jesus would respond to such loss, tragedy, suffering, and pain, because there are four books of the Bible written about how he did just that. And that is how my family and I (Eric) found an answer. We participated in the collection taken by our church. This past spring our church sent a team of medical and construction personnel to one of the villages hit hardest by the tsunami."

Touched by the images he saw on television following the tsunami, radio host and worship leader John Tesh couldn't simply sit and watch.[7] In the weeks following the tsunami, John and his family traveled across the world to help. Not knowing exactly what they could do to help, they landed in a Red Cross shelter area where hundreds of families, mostly children, were staying. John's son, Gibb, played soccer with the displaced children. His daughter, Prima, showed the young girls how to dance to American music. Those simple acts of sharing routine life again brought moments of laughter and small pieces of normalcy to a place filled with fear and despair. John's wife, Connie Selleca, pulled out crayons and paper. And the children of the tsunami began to draw. They drew amazing pictures of their families and the great wall of water that had changed their lives in an instant. John listened to the stories, over and over, from families who had been separated and lost everything. The stories, pictures, and compassion experienced during John and Connie's visit turned into a little book titled *Shades of Blue.* Back in the States, the book helped raise awareness of and funds for the children who experienced the disaster.

> *We are called to not only receive grace, but to be grace dispensers.*

But not everyone can respond in such a direct and generous way as the Tesh family. What do you have to give? Consider the true story of a little girl who put all of her Christmas money in an envelope and brought it to church one Sunday following the tsunami. She gave it to a church usher and said, "I want this to help those kids on the other side of the world." We don't know her name or her age—we only know that she simply gave all she had.

GOD'S GIFT, YOUR GIFT

Salvation by grace through faith might be considered God's gift to you. The good that God prepared for you to do is your gift back to God and to the world. Peter Semeyn, senior pastor at Faith Reformed Church in Traverse City, Michigan, says, "Part of our conversion is to be shaped and formed to more perfectly reflect the image of Christ the rest of our lives. Part of that shaping is to respond in heart, mind and deed as Christ would respond. That is our testimony. No change has taken root in our lives until it is given an outward expression. We are called to not only receive grace, but to be grace dispensers."[8]

Another way to look at the first aspect of your story (what God saved you *from*) is to consider this: if you were to die tonight, do you have the assurance that you are going to Heaven? Here is what Paul says about this: "Saving is all his idea, and all his work. All we do is trust him enough to let him do it. It's God's gift from start to finish! We don't play the major role. If we did, we'd probably go around bragging that we'd done the whole thing! No, we neither make nor save ourselves. God does both the making and saving" (Ephesians 2:8-10, *The Message*). We can rest assured that God is able to save us.

The second part of your story (what God saved you *for*) asks something different. If you were not going to die for another fifty years, do you have a purpose big enough to carry you the distance? *The Message* describes it this way: "He creates each of us by Christ Jesus to join him in the work he does, the good work he has gotten ready for us to do, work we had better be doing" (Ephesians 2:10). Have you ever thought of yourself as a partner in the work God has for you? He has invited you to join him in the work he does!

FINDING YOUR SWEET SPOT

If you've ever played golf, you are probably familiar with the concept of the sweet spot. The sweet spot is that place on the club that wastes the least amount of energy when it comes in contact with the ball. When you hit the ball close to the sweet spot of the club, the club transfers more energy to the ball—resulting in a ball that goes long and straight. If the ball connects too far to the inside of the clubface, you hook the ball. If the ball connects with the outside of the clubface, you slice the ball too far near the bottom of the clubface and you top the ball, driving it into the ground. And if you connect with the top of the clubface, it sends the ball skyward. To connect at the sweet spot is poetry in motion and appears nearly effortless. Golfer Tiger Woods knows how to find that sweet spot.

Where is your sweet spot? It is at the intersection of two things:

1) Your passion—the way God designed you
2) God's purpose—the good works he prepared in advance for you to do

Your passion

The first component of the sweet spot is your passion—the way God designed you. You have been fashioned by God as a unique individual. There is no one like you. The artist Pablo Picasso, though not known for his faith, understood this concept of unique design very well. "My mother said to me, 'If you become a soldier, you'll be a general; if you become a monk, you'll end up as the pope.' Instead, I became a painter and wound up as Picasso."[9]

You have talents, abilities, passions, experiences, and relationships that are uniquely yours. The psalmist says, "You created my inmost being [*inner qualities of talent, strength, and disposition*]; you knit me together [*your outward body*] in my mother's womb." Then he bursts out, "I praise you because I am fearfully and wonderfully made" (Psalm 139:13, 14).

In 2001 Marcus Buckingham and Donald O. Clifton released a book entitled *Now, Discover Your Strengths*. The book is based on interviews conducted by The Gallup Organization with more than two million of the best "doctors and salespeople and lawyers . . . and professional basketball players and stockbrokers and accountants and hotel housekeepers and leaders and soldiers and nurses and pastors and systems engineers and chief executives."[10]

The focus of their interviews was discovering what made these people so good at what they did. In the course of the research, patterns began to emerge that led to defining thirty-four strength patterns of human talent. The authors note that the thirty-four patterns, or themes, are as complete as the eighty-eight keys on the piano. In the right combination, anything can be played. The point of the book is to learn to identify and capitalize on your strengths, not to try to fix your weaknesses. The authors define strengths as "consistent near perfect performance in an activity."[11] Strengths are made up of three components:

1) Knowledge—both factual knowledge and experiential knowledge
2) Skills—the defining steps of an activity
3) Talent—"any recurring pattern of thought, feeling, or behavior that can be productively applied"[12]

The authors point out, "Skills determine if you *can* do something, whereas talents reveal . . . *how well and how often you do it.*"[13] "Your talents are innate . . . whereas skills and knowledge can be acquired through learning and practice."[14]

What strengths do you bring to the table? What is your combination of knowledge, skills, and talents? How has God uniquely fashioned you to contribute to what he is about in this world? It is good to remember that most skills have a neutral moral quality to them. G. K. Chesterton said, "If a man were to shoot his grandmother at a range of 500 yards, I would call him a good shot, but not necessarily a good man."[15]

God's purpose

The second ingredient of the sweet spot is God's purpose—the good works that God prepared in advance for you to do. Remember, because they are *prepared* for you, they are yours to discover, not invent. God's creating you and his preparation of these good works for you go together.

In the New Testament book of Acts, Peter says about the life of Christ, "God anointed Jesus of Nazareth with the Holy Spirit and power, and . . . he went around doing good" (Acts 10:38). Since Jesus' life was defined by doing good, his life can serve as a guide. So what were some of the good works of Jesus?

- He cared for the physical needs of people.
- He fed people who were hungry.
- He helped at a wedding.
- He alleviated suffering.
- He served others.
- He restored people to wholeness.
- He prepared people for eternity.
- He did anything that advanced the will of God in the lives of others.

We give hands and feet to the words of Jesus when we engage in doing good to others. Sometimes that service comes in unlikely packages.

> *We give hands and feet to the words of Jesus when we engage in doing good to others.*

Clay loves chain saws. You might say that Clay's passion is chain saws. As a concert pianist's hands are blessed with long fingers to reach all of the keys, Clay's hands are made to hold a chain saw. Since he's a contractor by occupation, chain saws are part of his vocation. To hold a humming, air-injected, nonvibrating, Model 340 Husqvarna chain saw is a dream come true. So when a call went out for people capable of running chain saws to cut up fallen trees after Hurricane Katrina, Clay's palms started sweating.

These words were music to Clay's ears: "And if the chain saw breaks, we'll have another for you. We've got chain saws . . . we need people to run them." The thought of being on the working end of a chain saw for an eighteen-hour stretch absolutely invigorated him. His passion intersected with God's purpose.

I once heard John Eldredge say, "Don't ask what the world needs. Ask what makes you come alive, and go do it. Because what the world needs is people who have come fully alive."[16] Clay is fully alive and feels God's pleasure as he works the chain saw.

GET BUSY

Take a look at your life story. There is never anything wasted in God's economy. Your story was not thrown together without a plan. Signing up for a life on loan from God means that you understand that your money and things are on loan, that your time and talents are on loan, and that your life experiences are on loan—all to be used to further his plan in the world.

You may have to "test drive" several opportunities before you find your sweet spot. But don't give up. Just get started. A friend noted that service, ministry toward others, has always been part of the Christian's DNA, but most of the time it is a recessive gene in the gene pool! Wouldn't it be wonderful if it were a dominant gene?

You are never too old to make an impact for Jesus. We like to think that the best years are still ahead of us. It's true, you know. As a follower of Christ, you can live with the conviction that the best years are still ahead of you, up to and including the day you die.

Benjamin Franklin, who (among other things) brokered France's help in our Revolutionary War at the age of seventy-six, went to France with the expectation of accomplishing something great. He felt that life, like a play, should end with the best act. An author and business guru once asked Peter Drucker (recognized as the Father of Modern Management) which of his twenty-six books he was most proud of. The eighty-five-year-old Drucker responded, "The next one."[17]

Peter Drucker gives us a challenge in our quest for leaving our mark: "The critical question is not, 'How can I achieve?' but 'What can I contribute?'"[18] What will *your* contribution be? What were you saved for? Go do it!

WHAT ABOUT YOU?

1. What are the things you sometimes try to fit into the God-shaped vacuum of your life?

2. Have you ever had an experience in which your passions intersected with God's purpose and you felt fully alive? What was it like?

3. What are your passions and skills?

4. Do you prefer working with people or working with your hands? Why?

5. As you look around your community, where do you think Jesus would go? What would he do?

6. How can you use your passions, skills, and talents to give hands and feet to what Jesus would do?

INTERSECTIONS

"You are the salt of the earth," Jesus told his followers (Matthew 5:13). Salt not only adds flavor to food, but it also serves as a preservative. Humans and animals need salt to survive. And Jesus let it be known that his followers were this very salt.

Jesus also told his followers, "You are the light of the world" (Matthew 5:14). Both salt and light are agents of influence, not agents of power or control. Influence is the ability to produce an effect seemingly without any direct or apparent effort. In calling us "salt" and "light," Jesus was defining our incredible power to intersect others' lives.

In this same Matthew 5 passage, Jesus tells us how we lose our influence—by losing our saltiness or by hiding our light under a "bowl" (v. 15). This can happen when we "hide" within the confines of our church or Christian community; we may be avoiding the very intersections God has brought our way.

If you open your eyes . . . wherever you are . . . and use your intersections for his glory, your influence has the power to change the ending of another person's story.

4

OPEN YOUR EYES

We must not, in trying to think about how we can
make a big difference, ignore the small daily differences we
can make which, over time, add up to big differences
that we often cannot foresee.

—MARIAN WRIGHT EDELMAN

My (Rick's) driver's education teacher was an interesting person. In the classroom and outside the vehicle, he was a nice man. In the car, though, he would yell for no apparent reason. I am sure this was some teaching technique he developed that had something to do with preparing students for the actual driving test for our licenses. One time as I approached a stop sign, he yelled at the top of his lungs, "Watch out for that stop sign!" His roar startled me so much that I hit the gas instead of the brake and flew through that intersection. Fortunately, he didn't yell at me very much after that.

To be honest, I don't really remember much from driver's ed class, except one thing that instructor kept repeating. That one thing has stuck with me all these years and still influences the way I drive today. "Always watch out for the intersections, Rick. Good things and bad things can happen at intersections."

That's exactly God's message to you: pay attention at the intersections. Keep your eyes open and look at what might be going on when you cross paths with another person. It's possible that God may have been planning for one of those good works he "prepared in advance" for you to do. Good things and bad things can happen at intersections. Maybe God is intending for you to arrive at an intersection at the same time another person is arriving—a person who might need exactly what you can do. I know there are times when I've approached such an intersection and, unfortunately, have gone blazing right through with my focus solely on myself and my agenda. Perhaps you have managed such occasions better. Or were you too busy or preoccupied to notice anyone or anything? That's easy to do—too easy, in fact.

Good things and bad things can happen at intersections.

FOCUS ON WHAT MATTERS

We live in a time when people are very preoccupied. Today's culture invites us, trains us, and encourages us to keep our attention on what we need to be satisfied or happy. Is too much of your life spent on your pursuit of the stuff that will satisfy? We are preoccupied with *more.* Our consumer mentality invites a constant dissatisfaction with what we have, and we search for something bigger or better.

A long time ago, a person could go to a convenience store and purchase a soda in a twenty-ounce cup. Twenty ounces seemed OK until the mid-1970s when 7-Eleven introduced the Big Gulp (a thirty-two-ounce drink). These days the most popular seller is sixty-four ounces. Bigger seems better, but did you know that the human bladder can hold only thirteen and a half ounces of liquid? What are we going to do with the other fifty and a half ounces of that Dr Pepper? You can super-size your dinner and eat it in front of your big-screen TV while you flip through hundreds of channels. In today's culture you and I eat megameals, drive megacars, shop in megastores, and attend megachurches. We have this appetite for more and are convinced that, somehow, bigger is better.

Consumer culture also tells us that, along with our preoccupation with more stuff, we need more activity—more things to do, more places to go, more people to impress. We are obsessed with greater achievements and better products, which take the shape of fun, money, toys, hobbies, relationships, jobs, accomplishments. . . . The list is nearly endless. Most of us keep trying to shove things into the vacuum in our lives with the expectation that we will be at peace and we will be happy. Peggy Noonan (former speechwriter for both presidents Reagan and Bush) says, "We are the first generations of man that actually expected to find happiness here on earth, and our search for it has caused such—unhappiness."[1]

We are so preoccupied with more that we can often lose sight of *most*. In the search for more, better, and greater, we forget to look at what God says is most, best, and greatest. The most beneficial thing we can do in this life is to find God and love him. Jesus said, "Love the Lord your God with all your heart and with all your soul and with all your mind. This is the first and greatest commandment" (Matthew 22:37, 38). The next best thing, Jesus said, is to love one another. "And the second is like it: 'Love your neighbor as yourself'" (v. 39). In Matthew 20:26, 27 Jesus summed up what it means to love God and to love people: "Whoever wants to become great among you must be your servant, and whoever wants to be first must be your slave." He said those words to his friends after the mother of two of them had just tried to secure a seat for her sons next to Jesus in his heavenly kingdom.

Not only did Jesus *say* those words to his friends, he also *showed* them what he meant when he washed their feet. You see, Jesus didn't just tell us how to think and act, he acted on what he said.

See the world's wonders

What happens if we stay preoccupied with more? We will become disappointed. God promises that nothing in this life will satisfy us completely. I'll always remember the first time I learned a little bit about that kind of disappointment. Every summer, Syracuse, New York, hosts the New York State Fair. Growing up in Syracuse meant there were plenty of trips to the fair with my parents and my sister, Darcy. As you might imagine, my parents actually wanted to tour through some of the exhibits— and see things like the World's Largest Butter Statue or New York's Largest Pumpkin. Darcy and I hated that stuff. We came for the Midway and the rides! Darcy loved the rides, and I loved the carnival games.

I was also intrigued by the large tent near the back of the Midway. It was decorated with amazing pictures of the World's Greatest Wonders. There was a toothless old man in a straw hat who invited us to come and witness the oddities. There was the alligator man, the bearded woman, the chicken-faced boy (my friends said *I* was the chicken-faced boy), and other amazing things. Tickets into the tent were only two dollars. The old man said that for a mere two dollars, I could gaze on these marvels from around the world. Every year I begged my dad to take us into the tent, and every year my dad said it was a waste of money. "All that stuff is just a hoax, and you will be disappointed."

I was in the seventh grade when my parents first let me go to the fair without them. They dropped my three friends and me off at the gate. You guessed it—we buzzed right past the butter statue and headed straight for the Midway. My friends got in line for the newest roller coaster, and I headed right to the World's Greatest Wonders tent—same toothless old man, same straw hat, same invitation—only now admission was four dollars (inflation I guess). I went to the window, bought my ticket, and got in line. The closer I got to the entrance of the tent, the faster my heart was beating—nerves and anticipation were about to do me in. Several times I felt so overwhelmed that I almost got out of line, but clutching my ticket in my sweaty palm, I wasn't about to miss what I had spent a lifetime wanting to see.

I wasn't in the tent five minutes before I was disappointed in what I was seeing. The "wonders" weren't even a good attempt at fakes. My dad had been right, and I was four dollars poorer.

We can spend a lifetime going up to the window and paying four dollars, convinced that this or that is going to fill the empty spot in our lives—only to walk away time after time, disappointed and just a little poorer. God's invitation to us is to discover him, to find purpose, meaning, wholeness, and peace in him, and to allow his story to change our stories. Yet most of us keep chasing after all kinds of other things that we are convinced will be just what we need to make our lives work.

What have you been chasing after so hard that has kept you preoccupied and kept you from seeing what God has in store for you?

See God's amazing grace

At the height of its conference attendance, Promise Keepers generated quite a bit of interest from the media. From a news media perspective, the events were unique or just plain weird. I happened to be at the Denver conference in Mile High Stadium where more than seventy thousand men showed up for the two-day conference. Among the media teams was a crew from the news and entertainment show *Turning Point*.

Maria Shriver was there to do an interview with Coach McCartney, the founder of Promise Keepers. She was also trying to catch a sense of what this cultural phenomenon was all about.

On Friday evening the worship leader had all seventy thousand men on their feet singing "Amazing Grace." I was seated along an aisle when I noticed a bit of commotion behind me. The director and crew from *Turning Point* were rushing toward the front of the stage to capture some of the footage during this song. Hearing seventy thousand men sing "Amazing Grace" was amazing! As the director was running past my seat, she turned toward the camera crew and said, "If we don't get this, we are dead."

Have you opened your eyes to the fact that your story is part of a much bigger story that God is writing?

I knew what she meant. Her producers would be upset if they failed to get that footage and missed a great shot to use as filler for the news story. It would play very well and capture the scene for their show. I couldn't help but think, though, that she was right in more ways than one. If we don't get God's amazing grace, if we miss out on his love, if we don't hear his story, then we miss out on the one thing that can bring to life what is dead or missing within us.

WHAT DO YOU SEE?

If you have opened your eyes to God's amazing grace and are trying to be less preoccupied with the stuff of life—then what? Accept his grace and extend it to others. In doing so, you see where God is working in your life and how his larger story is being written. When you come to an intersection, look both ways—up and out! Keep your eyes open and look at what might be going on when you cross paths with another person. Have you opened your eyes to the fact that your story is part of a much bigger story that God is writing? There are things God is planning for you and counting on you to do as a result of experiencing his love in your life.

I often wonder how many good things I've missed that were planned for me to do. As I've cruised through the intersections of my life, I'm sure I've missed out on some of the good works God had planned in advance. There have been too many times when I've been focused on what I am doing or caught up in whatever is going on in my life at the moment. I've missed opportunities to do good—to help write the story. Have you ever been so focused on yourself or something in your life that you didn't even notice the other people all around you or in front of you—much less make an effort to help meet their needs? It's time to pay attention.

Do you see this woman?

In Luke 7 Jesus was invited to have dinner at Simon's home. Simon was one of the religious leaders of his day, and it would be no surprise that he would want to connect with Jesus. After all, Jesus was getting a lot of attention from the locals—with the way he taught them about God, the miracles he performed, and his claims of being the Messiah. So Jesus and Simon got together for a meal. During the meal a woman who didn't have the best reputation in town came into the room. She began to wash Jesus' feet. Her tears and an expensive perfume she had brought served as the water; she used her hair as a towel.

This tremendous act of respect and devotion was impressive—especially since it wasn't this woman's job to be washing someone's feet. It was the custom of the day to wash the feet of a guest who had traveled on dusty roads to arrive at your home. That act was a normal way to show respect for the guest of honor. Somehow Simon didn't get that accomplished, and the woman, in humble respect for Jesus, paid him this great tribute.

Simon was looking at this spectacle and thought to himself, *"If this man were a prophet, he would know who is touching him and what kind of woman she is—that she is a sinner"* (Luke 7:39). In other words, Simon thought that Jesus should boot her out on the street or yell and embarrass her somehow. Jesus responded to his thoughts. (Kind of scary to have that happen, wouldn't you say? What if Jesus were to respond to what you are thinking right now?)

We view others in terms of their weaknesses, and we see ourselves in terms of our strengths.

Jesus told Simon a story about people who owed money. One person owed a little money, and the other owed a lot. Both were forgiven of their debts. Jesus asked Simon, "Who do you think is more grateful?" Simon answered, "Probably the one who owed the most money." Jesus told him he was exactly right. "Then [Jesus] turned toward the woman and said to Simon, 'Do you see this woman?'" (Luke 7:44). This wasn't some kind of eye test, like "Can you see the big *E* on the wall?" It wasn't even a challenge to see if Simon would acknowledge the woman's presence. Jesus was asking Simon what he saw. Did Simon see *this woman* or only her faults? Did he see *her* or the stuff in her life that he didn't like? Did he see *the person* or her issues? What did Simon *see?*

I understand Simon. I can be like him at times. You probably can relate as well. We view others in terms of their weaknesses, and we see ourselves in terms of our strengths. At times we just don't see other people at all because we are blinded by our own issues, our own agendas, and our own plans.

Do you see Joey?

His name was Joey and nobody liked him. My friends and I didn't like him either. It was easy not to like him. He didn't fit in socially, and he was awkward physically. He was also pretty grubby looking. Joey didn't seem very bright, and he certainly wasn't athletic. He sat alone at lunch and stood by himself on the playground. We were fifth graders and just plain mean; somebody had to be the person that no one liked. Joey was the easy target, and I jumped right in with everyone else when it came time to pick on him. Most of the time, though, I just didn't see him.

Through my adult years during my visits back home, I have looked for Joey's name in the phone book to see if I could find him. I've asked friends if they know where he is. On the other side of fifth grade, I recognize now that there were, more than likely, some things going on in Joey's life that contributed to the way he acted. I have tried to find him simply to say "I'm sorry. I'm sorry I just didn't see you. All I saw were things about you that made you easy to pick on." I'd like to tell him about my story and tell him that we all have weaknesses and flaws and issues and hurts. I'd like to see Joey . . . really *see* him.

CHECK YOUR EYESIGHT

How about you? Who are you not seeing? Jesus was asking Simon if he could see this woman as a little girl who used to love to laugh and play. Could he see some of the hurts in her life? Could he see a teenager with so much potential but no one to encourage her? Could he see that she was confused and making some poor choices? Could he see the woman whose heart had been chipped away at and now was much harder than she wanted it to be? That is what Jesus saw in the woman who washed his feet with her tears. How would you have seen her?

Gorillas in our midst

In February 2004, *Scientific American* published an article on what is called inattentional blindness, about an experiment conducted by the Visual Cognition Lab at the University of Illinois.[2] The subjects watched a one-minute video of two teams of three players each. One team wore black shirts and the other team wore white shirts, and the players moved around one another in a tight circle, tossing two basketballs. The subjects were asked to count the number of passes made by the white team—not an easy task given the interweaving movement of the players. After thirty-five seconds and out of the blue, a gorilla entered the circle, walked directly into the midst of the weaving players, thumped his chest, and nine seconds later exited out of the circle and out of view.

Now here's the amazing part. A full 50 percent of the subjects didn't see the gorilla! They were so caught up in counting the passes that they never saw the gorilla!

Are you so focused on whatever task is at hand that you are missing out on what is going on around you? What would happen today, this week, this year, if you were to see the people around you . . . *really see them?* Look at the people in your home, not at their issues. Look at the people at work, regardless of your connection or network. See the people you pass on the street, in a store, or at the gas station. You may not like some of their choices or their actions, but do you see what God sees in each of those people?

When you begin to see *people,* it may cause you to redefine what faith is. When we love God and love (see) our neighbors, it's only another small step to serving them—putting action to our faith. Here is a biblical truth:

you will never, ever lock eyes with anybody who isn't valued by God just as you are valued by God, no matter what his or her life looks like.

Be warmed . . . be filled

The book of James presents an interesting challenge for us to consider: "Does merely talking about faith indicate that a person really has it? For instance, you come upon an old friend dressed in rags and half-starved and say, 'Good morning, friend! Be clothed in Christ! Be filled with the Holy Spirit!' and walk off without providing so much as a coat or a cup of soup—where does that get you? Isn't it obvious that God-talk without God-acts is outrageous nonsense?" (James 2:14-17, *The Message*).

What would happen today, this week, this year, if you were to see the people around you . . . really see them?

Nancy is a Christian who knew this Bible passage in James. She even went to a Christian college. She remembers a campus joke she and her friends had about the verse. "We know-it-all students used the verse to tease other students who came into our dorm hall and asked for help. 'Anybody wanna give me a ride to work?' 'No, but be warmed, be filled, go in peace.' 'Can someone lend me some money?' 'No, but be warmed, be filled.' We seemed to delight in showing our friends that we could quote the Bible, but we weren't all that interested in lifting a finger to help them."

Then Nancy had an experience that reminded her vividly of James's illustration. It started as a simple prayer request. Nancy is on a prayer team at her church. This team prays for all of the requests written down on little white cards her church uses to track addresses, visitor information, and congregational prayer requests. The requests get divided up among the staff and others. One particular week, a prayer request seemed rather urgent to Nancy. She shares, "I tried to contact the woman by phone, but her phone was disconnected. So I decided to write her a note of encouragement and drop it by her house."

When Nancy drove up in front of the woman's house, she saw smashed pumpkins on the driveway, trash cans dumped over, and lots of egg yolks running down the side of the house. "I had to be careful where I walked as I went to the front door." She tucked the note inside the screen door and prayed that this woman's problems would be resolved. "As I drove away, I wondered how long it would be until she came home from work. I wondered whether it would be too dark for her to notice my little card. I wondered if she would see the smashed pumpkins or trip over them." Nancy's car slowed down as she came to the realization that leaving the card inside the woman's door was like saying to her, "Be warmed, be filled, go in peace."

Nancy found herself at one of those life intersections. At all intersections there are choices to make. "I had planned to run some errands, but somehow my car ended up back in my driveway. I changed my clothes and gathered a bucket, some rags, and a scrub brush. I prayed that there would be a hose and a faucet outside her house, as I got back into my car to return to her house." She rehearsed a speech in case the woman had arrived home. Nancy and the woman didn't know each other, but she was going to clean off her door, porch, and driveway anyhow.

With still no one home and the sun beginning to set, Nancy began cleaning. Suddenly, the next-door neighbor and three young boys joined her. "I began explaining that I didn't really know this woman, but I didn't want her to have to come home to such a mess," Nancy says.

"We'll help," the neighbor said. She sent the kids in for a trash can and some shovels. "I don't know why I didn't think of doing this," she admitted to Nancy.

Well, it wasn't my first thought either. Nancy recalls, "Even after seeing the mess, I just planned to deliver my prayer note and head on my way. I'm really thankful that God's Spirit nudged me (well, truthfully, more like clobbered me) so I wouldn't miss the opportunity to demonstrate my faith."

Did the woman who was helped ever respond to the generosity of neighbors and strangers? The answer is yes. But the point of this story is not about that response. The point is about Nancy's response. "On that day I realized that if I just left my note and drove away, I would be living a hollow and shallow faith. I had to take the next step. Whether or not she ever thanked me, I needed to clean her porch simply as an offering to God for how he has blessed my life."

Was Nancy's good deed a way to get her into Heaven? Is there a colossal scoreboard tracking who is leading the charge in good deeds to be first in line for Heaven when the doors open? No. God's gift of salvation is . . . a gift. It's free. You cannot earn it. If you have accepted that gift, you have discovered his grace because you recognize that none of us is worthy of it. You'll naturally begin to live your life differently. If you say you are a follower of Christ, and that you have faith, then the Bible says you are God's workmanship—you are a life on loan from him to do good things that God has already prepared for you to do. If you have tasted God's grace and love, then good news and good deeds go together. They are hand and glove.

Have you ever had an experience like Nancy's? Have you ever realized that you need to take the next step and get involved in someone else's messy life? If you keep your eyes open, the opportunity is sure to come.

LIVE IN THE MOMENT

His name was Dr. Lester Ford, and he was, by far, the kindest and most gracious person I (Rick) had ever met. Dr. Ford was a gentleman in every sense of the word. He had been a civil engineer, a minister, and a college president. He was seventy-five when I first met him. (Looking back, I assume someone must have been paying him to spend time with me just to see what he could do with a lump of clay.)

At this time Dr. Ford, long retired, was living in Ft. Myers, Florida. My wife and I had just moved to Ft. Myers from New York to begin a ministry position. We had mixed emotions about this move so far away from our first apartment, our best friends, and both our families. To make matters worse, we had left on my wife's birthday. Somewhere around Atlanta, Diane quit crying, and just north of Tampa she spoke to me again.

Live in the moment and give all you have— your energy and your effort—to what you are doing right now.

One day at lunch Dr. Ford asked me, "Rick, what are some of your dreams?" As a young man who had just moved to begin a new career, I had lots of dreams and began to share them with him. As I told him the things I wanted to do someday, he listened carefully. He nodded in agreement with some of my plans, some he smiled at, and a few seemed to take him back to another time and place. When I finally finished my list, he leaned across the table and said, "Rick, it is a good thing for you to keep dreaming. Always have a dream. Ambition can be good if you don't lose your focus and you keep God in view."

Then he spoke words that literally changed my life: "With all those dreams, don't forget to be of value where you are. Don't worry about being of value where you aren't yet!" In other words, live in the moment and give all you have—your energy and your effort—to what you are doing right now. Invest in the place where God has you at this moment, and don't spend the best of yourself being where you aren't.

That is what it means to live a life on loan—to live your life, with God's grace, right where you are. Give your very best—right now, in this place, to this situation. Don't get so caught up in the future that you miss the present.

In many ways, that line of thinking can be hard because it is a no-excuses policy for life. It takes away the ability to make excuses for poor results. You know the ones: "If only I was in a different place, worked with different people, had different circumstances, had a better marriage, had more money, and my childhood hadn't been so difficult." Have you ever allowed poor performance or laziness to be covered over by some excuse? A lot of Christians have even allowed lackluster effort to be glossed over in spiritual terms: "Well, I may not be Billy Graham, but I sure am faithful." Elton Trueblood is credited with saying, "Holy shoddy is still shoddy."[3]

Your life matters, and your choices have an impact. What you choose to do and how you choose to live can make a difference. Dream, plan, and invest in the future, but live in this moment.

GUIDELINES FROM AN APOSTLE

One of Jesus' first disciples, Peter, gave good instructions on how to live wherever we are right now.

The end of all things is near. Therefore be clear minded and self-controlled so that you can pray. Above all, love each other deeply, because love covers over a multitude of sins. Offer hospitality to one another without grumbling. Each one should use whatever gift he has received to serve others, faithfully administering God's grace in its various forms. If anyone speaks, he should do it as one speaking the very words of God. If anyone serves, he should do it with the strength God provides, so that in all things God may be praised through Jesus Christ. To him be the glory and the power for ever and ever. Amen (1 Peter 4:7-11).

As Peter wrote these words, he was near the end of his own life, and he wanted to remind us that our life choices matter. These words sound a lot like Dr. Ford's "Be of value where you are!" All of the imperatives in Peter's challenge are choices we get to make. You can choose to love even when people are unlovable. You can choose to serve even when you feel like you're the one who should be served. You can choose to give when you'd rather keep. Peter had seen firsthand how grace can show up and make a difference. He had personally experienced change.

The end is near

A priest and a rabbi who lived in the same neighborhood were putting a sign along a curve in the road near their homes. The sign said "The end is near. Turn back." As they were pounding in the last post, a car screeched to a stop just past the sign. The driver backed up, rolled down his window, and shouted to the priest and rabbi, "You people drive me nuts! Why are you always trying to scare people to get them to believe in God? Keep your views to yourself!" He went roaring off and left the priest and rabbi in a cloud of dust. A few seconds later, the priest and rabbi heard a loud crash. The rabbi said to the priest, "Maybe we should have just made the sign say 'The bridge is out.'"

Is Peter using a scare tactic with the "end is near" statement? Is he saying "turn or burn"? Not exactly. He is saying that God has done everything he said he would do. He has fulfilled every promise he has given. It is finished. Any moment could be the moment when God says "Enough." With that in mind, Peter is reminding you to live every moment in such a way that God is honored and that your moments are used to help write God's story in the lives of others.

Be clear-minded and self-controlled

Peter knew that it takes more than good intentions to make our moments count. As well-intentioned as he was, Peter couldn't keep himself from blowing it sometimes. When Jesus told his disciples that one of them was going to betray him, Peter answered that it wasn't possible that he would be the one. Peter would fight to the death; he could be counted on. Early the next day, Peter found himself on three occasions denying he ever knew Jesus. When Jesus needed a friend—someone to stand there—he had no one, including Peter.

I wonder if it wasn't this moment that Peter reflected on as he sat with his pen in hand, writing—thankful that God is in the business of fixing the holes in our hearts. Peter wasn't always clear-minded and self-controlled; look at all that happened in his life even after his disappointing choice to deny Jesus. Peter's life is a testimony of what can happen because of grace.

It is likely that along your life's journey, you have experienced some difficult trials, and maybe some of them have been tragic. Some may have been the result of the choices another person made, and some may have been the result of your own choices. As hard as you might try, you cannot control all of the circumstances in your life. You do, however, have the opportunity to control your responses and your attitudes. You get to choose how you shape your moments or whether you will allow the circumstances to shape you in negative or positive ways.

Is your past dictating your future? Do the elements of your past cause you to live in a fog and sometimes to live out of control with anger, despair, or bitterness? Peter says that you get to choose your response.

Another choice you get to make is whether to invite God into the moment . . . so that you can pray. You can choose to go it alone or allow God to be in the middle of your situation. Sure, you won't always make the best choices or always respond with grace, but when you invite God into the middle of your circumstances, he will help you with your attitude and responses.

Bob is a dear friend who reminds me a lot of Peter—and myself. At one moment Bob is saying the very words of God, and a moment later . . . well, you'll see what I mean. I had been driving down to south Denver for several months for a men's Bible study at a local restaurant. As we drank our coffee and sliced our ham and waffles, Bob excitedly shared, "This group has changed my life in two dramatic ways. First, I don't cuss or swear anymore. And second, when I used to come here, I was sort of embarrassed to be seen carrying my Bible, so I'd usually hide it under my coat. But now I just walk in, carrying it in my hand, and I don't give a @*&#?% what anybody thinks!" Like Bob and like Peter, our behavior sometimes still has to catch up with our beliefs!

> *Love people even though they are unlovable, unbearable, and undesirable. Why? Because there are times you are unlovable, unbearable, and undesirable—and God still loves you.*

Love each other deeply

This idea of love is much more than just some touchy-feely kind of thing. Loving each other deeply goes beyond the "Love makes the world go round" slogan. Love is about choice. Real love is a mental choice and an emotional commitment to care—even when we don't feel like it. Peter is saying to love people even though they are unlovable, unbearable, and undesirable. Why? Because there are times *you* are unlovable, unbearable, and undesirable—and God still loves you.

This kind of love calls you to something deeper than your natural response. It isn't easy to love people, especially people who have hurt you, betrayed you, or marked your life with their choices. When you choose to love this way, it isn't a statement like "I love you because. . . ." You are saying "I love you anyway."

JL joined the Marines right out of high school to get away and to get on with his life, to make something of himself, to get a fresh start. There was nothing in St. Louis holding him back—not his parents, his girlfriend, or the church in which he sometimes sat on Sunday mornings. He was leaving his past and building his future.

JL excelled as a Marine, graduating as the Company Honor Man in basic training, setting the range marksmanship record, and receiving a meritorious promotion. Intersecting with God's story wasn't part of JL's story, but all that was soon to change—by way of a one-hundred-thirty-five-pound corporal named Randy at JL's next duty station. As JL worked as company clerk in the famed Remington Raiders, Randy came by. Soon his story was intersecting with JL's story in such a way that God's story quickly became part of JL's story. He committed his life to Jesus Christ. Immediately, the two men began to reach out with the good news of Jesus to other Marines on the base.

One night Randy showed up at JL's door with his face swollen and bruised. When JL asked, "What the heck happened to you?" Randy replied that he was sharing Christ with a soldier in the next barracks and was beaten up in the process. But Randy didn't let that stop him. Shortly after JL was discharged from the Corps, he received a letter from Randy telling him some good news: the guy who had beat him up had come to faith in Christ. Now the two of them were sharing Christ with the other Marines. This is the I-love-you-anyway principle lived out at its finest.

Give hospitality without grumbling

Give hospitality. Maybe we all can find a way to do that, but do it without complaining? Now, why did Peter have to add that last part? Peter is getting to the heart of motive here. Ever been smiling on the outside while whining on the inside? The Greek word for *grumbling* means "to utter in a low voice or tone." What if you were to take some of your moments and simply find ways to happily offer real hospitality?

We can get a taste of what real hospitality is like by contrasting a couple of Scripture examples. In Luke 14:1-14, we find Jesus in the home of a Pharisee. Verse 1 says Jesus was the object of suspicion—"he was being carefully watched." And he wasn't treated very well in the rest of the chapter either. His hosts were grumblers. How different was Mary and Martha's behavior in Luke 10:38-42 when Jesus visited—they were listening to Jesus and preparing things for him.

But can something as simple as hospitality change lives?

In New York, Marie Rothenberg's ex-husband was supposed to take their six-year-old son David to the Catskill Mountains for an outing.[4] Instead, he excited David with, "I have plane tickets to California. I am going to take you to see Mickey Mouse in Disneyland." And off they went.

After checking into a motel not far from Disneyland, David's father gave David a sleeping pill and put him to bed. While David slept, his father bought explosive fuel and poured it over his sleeping son, the bed, and parts of the room; then he lit the fuel and raced out to the parking lot. The room literally exploded into flames. Some people heard David's screams, ran into the room, and carried out the near-dead boy. The fire burned away David's skin, hair, eyebrows, eyelashes, nose, lips, fingers, and toes.

News about this tragedy broke all over California, but no one knew the boy's identity. David's father contacted Marie with the news that David might be a patient in the University of California Irvine Hospital.

She called the hospital to ask if David Rothenberg was a patient there. At first, she got a negative answer. But because of the desperation in her voice, the telephone receptionist was keen enough to transfer her call to David's room. An attending nurse asked motionless David, "Is your name David?" There was enough movement that she said to Marie, "We aren't sure, but we may have your son here." After Marie flew to Los Angeles, arrived at the hospital burn center, and identified her son, the news media broke into all programs with the update.

Meanwhile, about twenty miles away, the Eastside Christian Church in Fullerton had just finished a jog-a-thon fundraiser to save Ken and Judy Curtis's house from being repossessed. Ken had spent many months without income while recovering from third-degree burns he sustained in an industrial fire.

As Ken and Judy were excitedly leaving the jog-a-thon that saved their house, they turned on the radio and heard a reporter announcing the identity of the boy and his mother. Judy remarked, "I know what she is going through and will continue to experience for months ahead."

Ken responded, "And I know what David is going through and will face in the future. Let's go see if we can help." They agreed, stopped the car, and prayed that they would be able to connect with Marie and befriend her.

People called it a miracle that Ken and Judy got into David's room without being stopped by law officers, who were stationed on all the hospital floors on the lookout for the father. Ken and Judy offered their house to Marie, along with a vehicle and meals, as long as she had need. For over a year, the Curtises were Marie and David's extended family and among their closest friends, along with a host of others in the church who also adopted Marie and David—loving them and meeting their needs in multiple ways.

Eventually both Marie and David became Christians because of the hospitality, friendship, and love of God demonstrated by God's sons and daughters in the Eastside Christian Church family.

Serve others by using whatever gift you have

Use whatever gift (or gifts) you have received to serve others. The implication is that you have something to contribute that will meet the needs of others. There is something tangible you can be doing, and in so doing, you are dispensing God's grace in a number of ways. This is how you manage what God has loaned you. How you act is a reflection on God—from the words you use and the way you live to the choices you make. You are either enhancing God's reputation or detracting from it. You are either dispensing grace or withholding it.

A good friend of mine penned these words as a worship song: "My life will be a story of your love. I'm a child of God and a reflection of . . . grace." It isn't enough for you to know what to do; it is the doing that matters. Knowledge is a good thing, but action is *the* thing. Thomas Huxley said, "The end of life is not knowledge but action."[5] It is one thing for you to know and understand the right stuff, but it is another thing for that understanding to show up in how you live. The toughest trip is from the head (knowing) to the heart (*really* knowing). But when that occurs, it can be seen in your hands (showing). God wants you to be his voice, his heart, and his grace lived out and extended to others. If you are a follower of Christ, this is exactly how God wants you to live.

If anyone speaks, if anyone serves

Peter said that we should speak as if speaking the very words of God. He said we should serve with the strength God provides. Why? So that God may be praised. You never know when a moment of significance will be coming your way.

Gordon is the facility manager for a large church. One of his routine jobs is to make sure everything in the building is up to snuff—including being ready when a fire inspector shows up unannounced.

And that is exactly what happened one day. Lon, a local fire inspector, showed up to inspect the building. Gordon's church was on his list of assignments for the week. It is never pleasant to be interrupted by any sort of inspection, but Gordon was always friendly, helpful, and honest with Lon when he came to visit. Gordon also happened to be a former emergency medical technician. With a lot in common and through the occasional inspection, Gordon was able to make a positive impression on Lon. So much so that Lon suggested to his wife that they visit the church. Eventually Lon and Sara found a place to call home.

How you act is a reflection on God— from the words you use and the way you live to the choices you make. You are either enhancing God's reputation or detracting from it.

If you catch yourself saying, "My life doesn't really matter, I don't have much to offer, and I can't make much of a difference," think twice. Being the facility manager doesn't always *feel* like ministry to Gordon. But any job, any task, and any moment can be used by God to create an intersection that will connect others to his grace. The biblical message is that God has a vested interest in you—how you speak and serve. God has plans for how his story is being written through your life. How you choose to intersect others' lives matters.

SEE AS GOD SEES

Paul Harvey always says, "And now, the rest of the story." While Lon and Sara's story is a nice story of a couple finding a church, that was just the beginning. Lon came from a family with a long medical history of ALS (Lou Gehrig's disease). As a thirty-one-year-old father of three young children, Lon found out that his particular case of ALS was an extremely aggressive kind. He would have only months to live. Was his family scared? Yes. Were they angry? Yes. But in knowing how many moments he might have, and by finding a church home, Lon found great insight into how God was writing a bigger story. Lon began writing and videotaping many, many messages. Here is some of what he shared with his family, friends, and church through a letter read at his funeral.

Most people look at my life and say it was way too short and that it's unfair. Some even get mad and wonder why I never got mad. My answer to this was always the same; first, I never had time to get mad. Mostly I would say that during this past year, I was just sad—sad for my kids, my wife, my family and friends. Not mad, just sad. As for fairness, well, I ask you this, "What is fair?" Is it fair for a mother and father to lose a newborn baby just minutes after birth? Is it fair for a man to live to be 100 years old only to outlive all his family and friends and the people who truly cared for him? What is fair?

Fair is this . . . God put each and every one of us on this earth to live a life according to His teachings, so that we may build a relationship with Him. Once this relationship has been created and our days here on earth are over, it will be because of Him that we get to go home. Fair is the fact that God gave us time on earth—how much time is up to Him. How you choose to use this time is up to YOU. Are you mad all the time? Do you worry about anything and everything? Do you take yourself too seriously? Take time to laugh and have fun!

I was just a guy, a father, a husband, a friend, a son, a brother, a cousin, a grandchild, and now I hope to be a fun memory for you!

Well . . . here we are. . . . I guess it's time to go home. Thanks, it's been fun!

Love forever and ever,

Lon[6]

It seems to us tragic that Lon's life ended so prematurely. But Lon had learned to see as God sees. He was a man who loved people, loved to laugh, and lived in the moment. He had discovered grace, and it was that grace that made a difference in how he faced his death.

The Smithsonian Institute has a display of eagles. They say an eagle has an innate sense of its impending death. It will leave its nesting place and fly to a solitary outcropping or precipice and land there. In that spot, the eagle will scratch its talons into the rock, face the rising or setting sun, and die. I've seen some eagles, like Lon Miller and Dr. Ford, who were fastened to the rock, faced the Son, and now are home.

At face value, neither having lunch with Dr. Lester Ford nor being kind to a building inspector is a significant thing. Then again, you never know how a simple moment may have a profound impact on another person. By choosing to open your eyes, to love, to invest, to extend grace, to serve, and to live in the moment—you can make a difference.

Looking to love

Cay Hood was her name, but everyone called her Mother Hood. She was a nurse at a home for the elderly and disabled for over twenty years. But this nurse was almost never off duty. Mother Hood would clock out but then not leave until she made sure everyone was settled in for the night. She retired once in 1982 but couldn't stay away for long. She went back after two years and began to volunteer. Always learning, growing, and maturing in her faith, Mother Hood volunteered to coordinate the chapel services at the nursing home as well as send greeting cards and call every member of her Sunday school class weekly to get a report on how they were doing. Even when she had to give up driving her 1968 Mercury, her days of serving were far from over. She would purposefully sit in the dining room of her assisted-living facility so that her chair faced the entrance. From that vantage point, she could watch for residents needing help. Her lifetime of serving others not only enriched her life but also created a legacy of faith for her children. Her son received awards for reading to the blind, and her two daughters served in nursing homes and churches throughout their lives. Mother Hood knew how to look for the needs God sees every day—and she was determined to do something about them. She was an ordinary person who was led and empowered by God.

Looking to extend grace

My wife and I (Rick) were sorting through some family albums, looking for a picture one of our kids needed. Of course, the mission of finding a picture gave way to reminiscing our way through several albums of family pictures. Most of those pictures were taken during vacations, birthdays, holidays, and events. As we turned through those pages, I caught myself starting to look at the photos differently. As Diane started some story or recalled some event, my mind was focused on the pictures with me in them. As the pages turned, I began immediately looking for myself in the pictures. I wasn't worried about what I looked like, but when I looked into my eyes, I wondered what I had been thinking when the picture was taken. I was looking to see if I was *there*. Of course, I was physically present in the picture, but where was I mentally and emotionally?

There have been plenty of moments when I stood smiling for a picture while my mind was in another place—thinking about work, cutting a deal, or preoccupied with one thing or another. And there were plenty of times on our vacations when you could find me trying to locate a spot where my cell phone worked. After all, there were things that needed to be done, and I needed to do them.

That night as we sat on the couch and looked at yesterday's pictures, I decided that in the future I want better pictures of myself. I want to be *there,* really *there* in each moment—enjoying the moment, utilizing the moment, capturing the moment, spending the moment, creating memories for that moment, being in the moment, and seeing the people who are with me in the picture.

All day long, every day, you have the chance to live in grace and extend grace, allowing God's grace to be seen in and through you. Does this mean that you have to get weird and walk around with a glow or halo around your head? No, of course not. (Well, maybe you could glow just a little.) But it does mean that you need to see people—really see people—as they cross your path. It means that you are cautious with your words, generous with your resources, and careful with your choices. It's paying close attention to people and circumstances in order to allow the good news you have discovered to show up in the good deeds you do. It doesn't necessarily mean you have to go across the world, but it could mean you need to go across the street. It doesn't necessarily mean you quit your job and become a full-time pastor, but it does mean that God sees you—and wants you to see yourself—as a minister wherever you might be.

Accepting God's gift of grace makes you an active part of his story, and there are real and relevant ways you can respond to his gift. There are needs all around you. Just be there . . . and open your eyes.

WHAT ABOUT YOU?

1. How has the push for more that dominates our society impacted you?

2. What are the "wonders" you have paid your four dollars for— hoping to fill an empty spot? Were you disappointed?

3. What are the reasons you often don't "see" the people around you?

4. How can you choose to live in the moment?

5. How can you use the gifts God has given you to extend his grace to others?

6. List some of the circumstances or people that have had an impact on your life intersections.

5
GRACE AT THE INTERSECTIONS

It seems people don't necessarily remember
what they are told of God's love, but they never forget what
they have experienced of God's love.

—STEVE SJOGREN

Ultimately God is interested in connecting each person with his story. If you have discovered God's story in a personal way, it is more than likely that introduction came through another person. A friend, neighbor, teacher, mentor, or family member probably helped you discover God's story. One person to another person—it's been the delivery method from the beginning.

Jesus' challenge to his closest associates was to "go and make disciples of all nations, baptizing them in the name of the Father and of the Son and of the Holy Spirit" (Matthew 28:19). We call this the Great Commission. If you are a believer and a follower of Christ, then God's invitation to you is to become a preacher. Now before you have a heart attack . . . a preacher is simply one who proclaims. While most of us see "preaching" as something only the minister does, the Bible says we are *all* ministers.

WHAT? ME A PREACHER?

The words *preacher* and *minister* are loaded words. Hearing these titles conjures up all kinds of images. Quite often these aren't the words that we want used to describe us. I (Rick) get that! I have been a minister for over twenty years and still don't like referring to myself as one, because it takes people a while to get past the mental images they have of preachers and ministers. Prior to moving to Colorado where I am the paid minister of a local church, I worked in administration at a small college and seminary. My sons were in first and second grades when we moved. On the first day of school, my oldest son was asked what kind of job his father had. He replied, "My dad used to have a job. Now he's just a minister at the church." From his vantage point, prior to moving I had a job with an office during the week, and on the weekends I preached for a new church plant. Now all I did was work at the church.

My son isn't the only one to think my job as a minister is just a Sunday job. One day Diane and I were eating out when a man came up and shared that he had been attending our church for a few months and that he really loved it. He said he was surprised he liked it because he had never been to church before. Then he leaned in and said, "If you don't mind me asking, I know you are busy on Sunday, but what do you do the rest of the week?"

I couldn't resist replying, "Well, you know, we have services on Saturday, so I am busy both Saturday and Sunday."

"Oh," he said, "that sounds like a great life." I decided not to try and explain it.

According to the Bible, if you are a follower of Christ, you are a minister, or preacher. So how is *your* preaching?

In this Matthew 28 command that Jesus gave his followers, he tells what to do (go into all the world and preach the gospel) but not how to do it. He leaves room for individual creativity. You have a responsibility to share the good news, but how you do that is entirely up to you. You get to choose the best way to communicate God's story. The message is the same—love, grace, and redemption through Jesus. That should never change. The methods through which that message gets delivered, however, are endless.

As you live your life on loan for God, serving him and honoring him, you will rub shoulders with others who do not believe. As a preacher you take your experiences, your personality, and your changed story and find ways to intersect others' lives and connect them to God's story. You are helping people change the endings to their stories, endings that are different from—and better than!—the endings they would have without God.

I've discovered in the ministry that the most effective message isn't the one delivered in a building to a group of people; it is the one that is lived day in and day out. When you ask people why they don't go to church, hypocrisy is the number one answer. Think about it. Why would someone want to be part of something that doesn't seem to have much effect on how people live? If people who say they know God's story don't act any differently than people who don't know his story, there is a huge disconnect. The message gets discounted without ever having a chance to be heard.

On a busy street, a cautious man was being tailgated by a stressed-out driver. Suddenly the light turned yellow in front of him. He did the vigilant thing, stopping at the crosswalk—even though he could have beaten the red light by accelerating through the intersection. The tailgater hit the roof—and the horn, screaming in frustration as he missed his chance to get through the intersection. As he continued ranting, he heard a tap on his window and looked up into the face of a very serious police officer. The officer ordered him to exit his car with his hands up. He took the man to the police station where he was searched, fingerprinted, photographed, and placed in a holding cell.

After a couple of hours, a policeman approached the cell and opened the door. The detained man was escorted back to the booking desk where the arresting officer was waiting with the man's personal effects.

> *The most effective message isn't the one delivered in a building to a group of people; it is the one that is lived day in and day out.*

The officer said, "I'm very sorry for this mistake. You see, I pulled up behind your car while you were blowing your horn, flipping off the guy in front of you, and cussing a blue streak at him. I noticed your Choose Life license plate holder, the What Would Jesus Do? bumper sticker, the Follow Me to Sunday School bumper sticker, and the chrome-plated Christian fish emblem on the trunk. Naturally, I assumed you had stolen the car."

You see, long before some people get to hear the Sunday morning message, they have been turned off by a few of the "messengers" they have met.

Conversely, when people allow God's love to be demonstrated in how they live, and when words and acts full of grace are evident, the opportunity to share the source of that grace is multiplied. Through your life on loan, you can earn the right to be heard. Your choices—how you choose to live out your story—speak loudly to people.

The pattern of people coming to Christ in the New Testament seems to be: (1) See, (2) Hear, (3) Believe. People observed something, which prompted them to listen to the accompanying message, and then (in many cases) they believed. If the pattern is seeing before hearing and hearing before believing, then we as believers must develop strategies for influence that let us show before telling.

WHAT IS EVANGELISM?

Evangelism is one of those big, scary, churchy words that may cause you to sweat, to feel unqualified and unsure. But evangelism is simply helping another person discover a different ending to his life story. Isn't that an incredible thought? When my (Eric's) kids were small, my wife and I read stories to them nearly every night. For a while, one of their favorite books was one that contained a succession of variable choices that led to different story endings. So if my kids followed one choice, the book instructed them to turn to such-and-such page where the story then picked up. Another choice took them to a different page. In that book the message was clear—choices determine outcomes. Often people conclude that their family histories, their setbacks, their successes, and their personalities have already determined the outcome of their lives. When you put your faith in Christ, everything changes. You now have hope. Every person's story can have a different ending.

Ready . . .

Evangelism is sharing that good news—a message that includes words of love combined with deeds of love, and deeds of love combined with words of love. In the Bible, the prophet Isaiah explained this idea.

> The Spirit of the Sovereign LORD is on me, because the LORD has anointed me to preach good news to the poor. He has sent me to bind up the brokenhearted, to proclaim freedom for the captives and release from darkness for the prisoners, to proclaim the year of the LORD's favor and the day of vengeance of our God, to comfort all who mourn, and provide for those who grieve in Zion—to bestow on them a crown of beauty instead of ashes, the oil of gladness instead of mourning, and a garment of praise instead of a spirit of despair (Isaiah 61:1-3).

Isaiah was called to preach, or communicate. How was the good news communicated? Through words of love ("proclaim freedom . . . release . . . the year of the LORD's favor") and deeds of love ("bind up the brokenhearted . . . comfort all who mourn . . . provide for those who grieve . . . bestow on them . . . beauty . . . gladness . . . praise").

Notice how this intersection of lives would change the ending to the story—comfort, beauty, and praise instead of mourning, grieving, ashes, and despair. God's story becomes their story. What is most interesting about these words from Isaiah is that they are also some of Jesus' first public words (see Luke 4:18-21). In Jesus' ministry, his good news would come in deeds of love and words of grace and truth (see John 1:14). His deeds of love would verify his words of grace and truth, and vice versa. It was often difficult to tell where his words ended and his deeds began or where his deeds ended and his words began. His *words* of love and *works* of love were seamless.

Aim . . .

In the 2004 Olympics in Athens, twenty-three-year old Matt Emmons of the U.S. shooting team was ready to shoot for his second gold medal.[1] Nine shots into the final round, he had a cushion of three points over China's Jia Zhanbo, his closest competitor. Matt set his sights on the target, took a breath, let it halfway out, and squeezed the trigger. Bull's-eye! Emmons waited for his score to appear on the monitor, but when his bull's-eye failed to register, he brought his complaint to the officials. The officials looked at his target. Mysteriously, Emmons's target on lane two was without a mark. But interestingly, the target on lane three had two holes in it! Emmons had shot at the wrong target in the finals of the Olympics and had to settle for eighth place.

As we seek to help people move toward Jesus, perhaps we need to rethink our aim. Steve Sjogren says,

Evangelism too often begins with an attitude of "ready, fire, aim." It seems to me, we have spent an enormous amount of time talking about changing the world, but little time actually doing much to bring about change. By redefining the beginning point of evangelism from speaking to showing God's love to the world, it's easy to launch out. As we serve the unchurched in small ways, with God's hand upon our lives, they will ask, "Tell me, why are you doing this?" No matter how strong our evangelism gifts, any Christian can answer the question.[2]

Steve is right. We can say without exaggeration that 100 percent of the time when you love, serve, and minister to others, sooner or later you will be asked "Why are you doing this?" That's when you must always, in the words of Peter, "be prepared to give an answer to everyone who asks you to give the reason for the hope that you have" (1 Peter 3:15).

Fire!

In the winter of 2005, I (Eric) was flying from Chicago to Denver. As the Boeing 777 reached cruising altitude, the purser made this announcement, "If you are sitting by a window, please lower your shades as it will enhance the beauty of our flight attendants." Sometimes things *do* look better with the shades drawn, but Christianity looks more attractive when the lights are turned on, as believers serve others with good deeds. If you are a believer in Jesus, are you helping Christianity look more appealing? Jesus said, "Let your light shine before men, that they may see your good deeds and praise your Father in heaven" (Matthew 5:16). Good deeds shine the light on the good news.

Good deeds also provide the evidence for the good news. Pastor John Bruce of Creekside Community Church in San Leandro, California, describes the vital link between word and deed. "For the longest time I felt like my evangelism was like presenting my argument before the jury—and the judge was not allowing me to present any evidence."[3]

Do you see what he was saying? No lawyer could ever get a conviction based on a linear verbal argument alone. There is always the need for evidence—Exhibit A, Exhibit B, Exhibit C. Serving others provides the evidence of what we are talking about.

There was an episode in Jesus' life when a paralyzed man was lowered through the roof by four of his friends so he could be in the presence of Jesus. The four friends believed Jesus could heal their friend. Jesus gave the best words of love a person can hear—"Friend, your sins are forgiven." When a few folks in the crowd got upset, Jesus responded, "That you may know that [I have] authority . . . to forgive sins . . . I tell you, get up, take your mat and go home" (Luke 5:20-24). It was his deeds of love that validated his words of love. Tim Keller, pastor of Redeemer Presbyterian Church in New York City, refers to deeds of love. He writes,

> Most Christians in evangelism seek only to make the gospel credible, to make it cogent and persuasive intellectually. But people believe in a message mostly for nonrational reasons. A belief appears convincing to the degree that it is supported by a consistent, loving group or community. . . . The ministry of mercy, then, is the best advertising a church can have. It convinces a community that this church provides people with action for their problems, not only talk. It shows the community that this church is compassionate.[4]

Your part, God's part

For many, prayer is an afterthought said over a meal or an utterance in times of desperation, like, "Lord, I *really* need a parking spot. Oh, never mind, I found one." But sincere prayer can put us in tune with what God is doing in a person's life and can create sensitivity to opportune moments.

Here's an effective question to ask yourself when you meet someone: *what is God doing in this person's life, and how can I help?* Keith Davy, longtime leader and educator with Campus Crusade for Christ, suggests you should pray consistently for three things in respect to telling your story to others:

1) Pray that God would prepare their hearts to believe the gospel (see Romans 10:1).

2) Pray that God would open doors for significant spiritual conversations with you (see Colossians 4:3).

3) Pray that God would give you the words to speak clearly as you engage with them in spiritual conversations (see Colossians 4:4).[5]

> *If people don't come to Christ through deeds of love, you should still continue with deeds of love because that's what you do as a Christ-follower.*

Of course, we'd love to see every person who is the recipient of deeds of love come to faith in Christ. But you don't need to display a false kind of mercy so that people will come to Christ; you simply show true mercy because God is merciful and you want to be like him. Unless you understand this, kindness, goodness, and mercy will be mere tactics of evangelism rather than a true reflection of who you are as part of God's story.

And if people don't come to Christ through deeds of love, you should still continue with deeds of love because that's who you are . . . that's what you do as a Christ-follower. Regardless of the outcome, recognizing that your life is on loan means that you will show love to people in practical ways—no matter what. Jesus placed value on people—people you and I would like to forget about: strangers, prisoners, the sick, the thirsty, and the hungry. He called them "the least of these" (Matthew 25:45). You extend grace and mercy because you are a Christian, not just so others will become Christians.

This is not to dull your passion for wanting people to come to Christ. Getting people into the kingdom should be your ultimate motive and hope. Your attitude should reflect Paul's when he said, "My heart's desire and prayer to God . . . is that they may be saved" (Romans 10:1). But it is Jesus who makes the permanent and eternal difference in someone's life.

SERVICE AT THE INTERSECTIONS

Good deeds (service) done selflessly toward others nearly always create goodwill with the recipients and those observing the intersection. Often after serving people in the community, the expressions of gratitude are awesome. In the Bible when Jesus healed or helped a person, the responses were expressions of goodwill—people were amazed, astonished, in awe, in wonder. Goodwill creates the platform to share the good news with others. Some intersections for service just naturally happen, and some you create.

One church we know of is partnering with an inner-city, public elementary school—providing after-school tutoring, winter coats, backpacks, school supplies, hosting teacher appreciation events, and more. When the school painted a mural on one of their walls, a third of the mural contained pictures of the church! Now that's pretty amazing! And it wouldn't have happened without good deeds that fostered goodwill, without individuals from the church (like you and me) picking up a paintbrush, purchasing a backpack, cooking a meal, or delivering a coat.

It was a July afternoon in the mountains of Colorado, and we were on a family vacation. I (Eric) was lying in a large hammock with my six-year-old nephew, Kyle. The hammock was slung underneath a porch that protected it from the falling rain. The rain was coming down fairly hard, and there were flashes of lightning and rumblings of thunder in the afternoon sky. Kyle lives on the California coast where thunder and lightning are rare. He had wanted to go swimming while it was raining, and I had just warned him of the lethal dangers of lightning. So as we swung in the hammock, I asked him some questions just to pass the time.

"Kyle, why did God make the trees?"

"Because he loves us," Kyle answered.

"Kyle, why did God make the grass?"

"Because he loves us," Kyle answered again.

"Kyle, why did God make lightning?"

"Because he loves us . . . and he wants to kill us!"

Creation is a great tutor to lead us to the creator, but it is a deficient teacher. We can get an incomplete picture of God by looking at creation alone, and we can come to erroneous conclusions about God. By his very nature God is a revealer. The Bible says that he reveals himself in creation (Romans 1:19, 20) and through the prophets (Hebrews 1:1), but his most complete revelation is Jesus. "The Word became flesh and made his dwelling among us" (John 1:14). There are places in the Bible that reference the fact that people are not able to see the invisible God. John

> *As followers of Christ, we each have the ability to make the invisible God visible by our words and our actions.*

says, "No one has ever seen God, but God the One and Only, who is at the Father's side, has made him known" (John 1:18). So it is Jesus who explains, by his teaching and action, what God is really like. John goes on to explain, "No one has ever seen God; but if we love one another, God lives in us and his love is made complete in us" (1 John 4:12).

It's when we love people that God's presence works in us and people get a better picture of God's love, mercy, and compassion. As followers of Christ, we each have the ability to make the invisible God visible by our words and our actions.

Actions open the door

When God is at work in general ways, people are left to their own current levels of understanding regarding what is happening. They depend on their own worldview and perception of reality to make sense of the story. When God's story specifically interrupts their stories, people ask themselves, *What is going on?* The conclusion is not always as intuitive as you might expect.

Even the followers of Jesus had experiences like this. When the early Christians came together after Jesus had gone back to Heaven, God intersected their stories by giving Christ's followers the ability to speak in unknown languages through a miraculous event on the Day of Pentecost. This action opened the door. Present that day were "God-fearing Jews from every nation under heaven" (Acts 2:5). The Bible records their response to God's intersecting with their stories: "When they heard this sound, a crowd came together in bewilderment, because each one heard them speaking in his own language. Utterly amazed, they asked: '. . . How is it that each of us hears them in his own native language?'" (Acts 2:6-8).

Amazed and perplexed, they asked one another, "What does this mean?" They saw, heard, and felt the evidence of God at work. Yet look at the words used to describe their level of understanding—"bewilderment" and "utterly amazed." And what did some in the crowd conclude? They said, "They have had too much wine." Their assumption was faulty; they interpreted these events through the lens of their own limited stories.

At this point Peter stepped in with God's story. He said to them, "Fellow Jews and all of you who live in Jerusalem, let me explain this to you; listen carefully to what I say. These men are not drunk, as you suppose. It's only nine in the morning! No, this is what was spoken by the prophet Joel" (Acts 2:14-16). Then Peter took the opportunity to tell them God's story, giving them not only an alternative explanation of the morning's events but also an opportunity to change the ending of their own stories. And the Bible records that "about three thousand were added to their number that day" (Acts 2:41).

Actions plus words

In the next chapter of Acts, Peter and John provide us with another illustration. Walking to the temple, they were intersected by a man disabled from birth, who was being carried by his buddies to the gate where he made his living as a beggar. When he extended his hand and asked Peter and John for money, Peter responded, "Silver or gold I do not have, but what I have I give you. In the name of Jesus Christ of Nazareth, walk" (Acts 3:6). You know what happened next? The man jumped to his feet, walking and praising God. How did the onlookers respond? Again, on their own they couldn't figure it out. Though the Bible says they were filled with wonder and amazement, the onlookers came to the skewed conclusion that the power to heal came from Peter and John, not God! In response, Peter was compelled to tell them the real story behind the story (see Acts 3:12-26). Several years ago, Christian statesman Elton Trueblood wrote,

> Testimony must be both deed and word. The spoken word is never really effective unless it is backed up by a life, but it is also true that the living deed is never adequate without the support which the spoken word can provide. This is because no life is ever good enough. The person who says naively, "I don't need to preach; I just

let my life speak," is insufferably self-righteous. What one among us is so good that he can let his life speak and leave it at that?[6]

In yet another incident, Paul and Barnabas entered the city of Lystra. There they met a man who had been lame from birth, and God (through Paul) healed him. No doubt this wonderful deed was a spectacle, but how did the residents of Lystra respond? Did they get it right? Did they become Christ-followers? Just the opposite! They shouted, "The gods have come down to us in human form!" (Acts 14:11), mistook Paul and Barnabas for Zeus and Hermes (quite a compliment really), and wanted to offer sacrifices to them. Initially, good deeds created goodwill but led to the wrong conclusions. Paul needed to add the words of the good news to complete the story.

Good deeds alone are insufficient to lead the curious to Christ. Steve Sjogren addresses this point by writing, "When we do speak we must be sensitive to the level of receptivity of each person and explain the words of God's love in whatever way the hearer can understand. These words are the cognitive or conscious element of our evangelism. If we don't follow our actions with words, they will only know that we are nice people, not that God loves them."[7]

The words clarify the actions

Good deeds create goodwill. But goodwill is not yet the good news. On Saturday afternoons, I like wandering over to Sam's Club for a little grazing. Scattered throughout the inner aisles of the store are employees handing out samples of foods—chicken tenders, breakfast burritos, Italian sausage slices, chips and salsa, taquitos, chocolate cake, beef stew, and power drinks. The food is very good, and the workers are very nice. But they leave nothing to the imagination as to why they are handing out free food—"We have a special on these today. The eight-hundred-twenty-ounce package of meatballs is only $9.95." Any curiosity I had regarding the samples is quickly answered. The workers' words explain their deeds; they want me to buy some meatballs.

The Bible says in the book of John that Jesus was engaged in miraculous signs—healing the sick, giving mobility to the lame, and restoring sight to the blind. This is the backdrop to Jesus' marvelous conversation with the scholar and religious leader Nicodemus. Nicodemus had observed the good deeds, but observation without explanation was insufficient. So he came to Jesus asking for more information. "Rabbi, we know you are a teacher who has come from God. For no one could perform the miraculous signs you are doing if God were not with him" (John 3:2).

All of Nicodemus's conclusions were correct but incomplete. Jesus had to bring good words to complement and complete his good deeds. What began with good deeds and created goodwill ended in very good news for Nicodemus. Lesslie Newbigin writes, "Almost all the great preaching in Acts is made in response to a question. Something has happened which makes people aware of a new reality, and therefore the question arises, What is this reality? The communication of the gospel is the answering of that question."[8]

BEING SALT AND LIGHT

Jesus' longest recorded speech is often called the Sermon on the Mount because he was teaching on a hillside. The people had gathered together below him to hear what this gifted teacher had to say about their lives and how they should live. They were hungry to hear how God loved them and wanted to reconnect with them. Jesus said,

> You are the salt of the earth. But if the salt loses its saltiness, how can it be made salty again? It is no longer good for anything, except

to be thrown out and trampled by men. You are the light of the world. A city on a hill cannot be hidden. Neither do people light a lamp and put it under a bowl. Instead they put it on its stand, and it gives light to everyone in the house. In the same way, let your light shine before men, that they may see your good deeds and praise your Father in heaven (Matthew 5:13-16).

Jesus is saying that if you are a person who has discovered God's love and grace in your life, you are a person of influence. Not that you could be, might be, should be . . . but that you *are*. Jesus compared you to salt and light. His questions are "What good is salt that loses its flavor?" and "What use is a light that is hidden?" Such salt and light have no influence.

> *A life lived as if it's on loan from God should be attractive and authentic.*

Salt and light make a difference in their surroundings. Salt brings flavor and light dispels darkness. Salt is a preservative. Light reveals what is hidden. In Jesus' day, both were precious commodities. Salt was often used to pay wages, conduct commerce, or close a deal. That is where we get the phrase "You're not worth your salt." Before electricity, light was more difficult to maintain or have in abundance, so it too was regarded as precious. Jesus used these two important but common elements to illustrate that a believer's life is useful and has influence.

Being salt and light at the intersections in life can have a huge impact on others. But what happens when we crash at the intersections and we aren't salt and light? Many times our involvement with others ends up with an adverse outcome. Mother Teresa wrote, "Often we Christians constitute the worst obstacle for those who try to become closer to Christ;

we often preach a gospel we do not live. This is the principle reason why people of the world don't believe."[9] To emphasize her point she noted, "Gandhi once said that if Christians lived according to their faith, there would be no more Hindus left in India."[10]

People most often interpret the validity of a person's beliefs by the attractiveness and authenticity of his life. A life lived as if it's on loan from God should be attractive and authentic. If your life is *attractive,* it means that you are living a bit more like Jesus lived. An *authentic* life means there is greater alignment between what you believe and the way you live. Some of the instructions from the Bible on how believers should live include the words "that in every way [we] will make the teaching about God our Savior attractive" (Titus 2:10). The way you live either validates or undermines the teachings of Jesus. At all times you are a living witness to what you believe. Others will draw their conclusions based on what they see in you.

Too much

Too little salt and the meal is bland; too much salt and the meal is ruined. I (Rick) found out just how powerful salt can be while sharing lunch with some family friends. It was a simple meal of sloppy joe sandwiches. As the platter passed by me, I was polite and took only one sandwich (but I planned on getting at least one or two more before the meal was done). I was into my third bite of the sandwich when I bit into something hard and crunchy. At first I thought it was a piece of burnt ground beef. The more I chewed, the worse it tasted. It was nasty! If I had been at home, I would have yakked it out onto the plate, but I chose to show some discretion with these friends we didn't see often. I started drinking as much water as possible and chewing until the thing could be swallowed.

When the platter came around again, it was easy to let it pass. About ten minutes later, my friend's five-year-old daughter started sputtering, gagging, and spitting out her food—which is exactly what I had wanted to do earlier. "Mom," she said, "this is horrible. It tastes awful." I was a silent sympathizer. Mom fished around on her plate and then announced to the rest of us, "Be careful. I put two bouillon cubes in the pan, and I guess they didn't dissolve." To which I replied, "It is safe to get back in the water—I already ate the other one." A whole bouillon cube in one bite!

Salt can help the flavor, but too much can destroy a meal. Light, like salt, must also be used with discretion. Too much light can be blinding. Sometimes Christians, having determined that more is better, use too much light. Sometimes even Christians with good intentions pile on the salt and turn up the light, as if shouting louder, emphatically drawing lines, and having a brighter spotlight are the way to show grace. Salt and light do come with warnings: Don't let the desire to influence be replaced with the need to control. Don't let the opportunity to impact be superseded by the desire to be right. Sometimes the message of grace and love is missed because the messenger has overwhelmed the receiver.

As a public school administrator, my friend Jack shared a little secret with me. He had not been interested in Christianity because most of the Christians he met through the school were yelling at him about all they thought was wrong. Interestingly, Jack found God's love and grace later in life through the quiet influence of other Christians who decided that serving in the public schools was a way to be salt and light.

Too little

The flip side of too much salt and light is that too little is not enough. Have you been a Christian for a while and lost your saltiness or hidden your light? I once had someone tell me he was a "stealth Christian"—that he didn't want to be obnoxious about his faith. The word *stealth* makes me think of the planes used in military maneuvers. The problem with being a stealth Christian is that no one knows whom you are flying for. We're here to be noticed. *The Message* version of our Matthew 5 passage hits home.

> You're here to be salt-seasoning that brings out the God-flavors of this earth. If you lose your saltiness, how will people taste godliness? You've lost your usefulness and will end up in the garbage. Here's another way to put it: You're here to be light, bringing out the God-colors in the world. God is not a secret to be kept. We're going public with this, as public as a city on a hill. If I make you light-bearers, you don't think I'm going to hide you under a bucket, do you? I'm putting you on a light stand. Now that I've put you there on a hilltop, on a light stand—shine! Keep open house; be generous with your lives. By opening up to others, you'll prompt people to open up with God, this generous Father in heaven (vv. 13-16).

Just right

How do you share Jesus Christ in a country where most of the ten million residents react with suspicion or see Jesus as just another way to "truth"? How do you reach those who see the church as a museum?

Pavel and Danka and their three children live in Europe in an eastern Czech Republic town called Ostrava, where they serve and lead in a local church. They seek out the needs of people, plan, pray, seek more, change plans, pray, and act. Establishing relationships and clarifying the gospel of Jesus Christ are their passions.

Prayer and creativity have led them to start small groups, lead open discussions, and present the truth of Jesus at several public events. For example, they presented a free public theater performance that focused on families and children and was filled with biblical truths. The main actor gave a personal testimony. Pavel and Danka have reached their community through helping repair and redecorate a local park and children's playground. For the past two Christmases, their church has reached a couple thousand people in the city through a public celebration of the birth of Jesus Christ. Their creativity in this situation used Czech birthday traditions to present the message of Jesus Christ.

People like Pavel and Danka give careful consideration to sprinkling on just the right amount of salt and shining just the right amount of light.

FINDING COMMON GROUND

Imagine Paul entering Athens in the first century. Overshadowing the city was the acropolis with its impressive Parthenon—a tribute to Greek ingenuity and their heroic gods. Paul did a bit of sightseeing, trying to discover his common ground with these Athenians. The Bible says that he "looked carefully at [their] objects of worship" (Acts 17:23). In the process, he came across an altar with the inscription To an Unknown God. So when he had the chance to speak to the Athenians about Jesus, he began with what he and they had in common: "I see that in every way you are very religious" (v. 22). In the midst of all the differences, he found a starting point—what he and they agreed upon—and he was able to tell them about Jesus: "Now what you worship as something unknown I am going to proclaim to you" (v. 23).

There is an interesting book on cross-cultural ministry called *Global Good News,* comprised of essays written by a variety of authors. One author offers particularly keen insight on areas that people of every culture have in common that can prove to be starting points of conversation. People talk easily about whatever makes them come alive, of course. Additionally, this author suggests some other conversation starters that he refers to as "universal languages":

- The care and concern for children
- Competitive sports
- Music
- The need for community
- The universal "oughtness"
- The telling of a "story"[11]

Does this get you thinking about how to start a conversation with people? You can find common ground, like Paul did, to begin any conversation that leads to sharing God's story. Eric Bryant, navigator (executive pastor) at Mosaic Church in Los Angeles, notes that the keys to evangelistic effectiveness are being "likable and accessible."[12] If you're not somewhat likable, people aren't interested in what you have to say. If you're not accessible, you won't have the time to spend together with those outside the faith.

In the summer of 2005, as part of National Trails Day, a few friends and I (Eric) helped build a trail on Davidson Mesa, overlooking the city of Boulder. A first-time experience for all of us, it was a good way to build community with our neighbors. It was the hottest day of the year (over ninety-five degrees), and we were pushing wheelbarrows up and down hills. It was dog-hard, arduous work that gave all of us great sympathy for those ancients who had built the Great Wall, the pyramids, and the Roman roads.

> *If you're not somewhat likable, people aren't interested in what you have to say. If you're not accessible, you won't have the time to spend together with those outside the faith.*

I wore a T-shirt with a picture of Olympic wrestler Dave Schultz, who was tragically killed in a bizarre murder a few years back. One of the people working with me saw my shirt and asked me about wrestling. He had wrestled in college, and when I told him I was a grappler as were both my boys, we became fast friends over this common ground. During the day we joked around and even locked up once or twice (you have to be a wrestler to understand this one).

By the end of the day, I was able to speak about some of my passions—engaging the church's needs and sharing dreams for the community. He responded by telling me he was on the board of a large human-service agency that was looking for ways to engage the faith community in its work. Imagine that! How different it may have been had I worn a T-shirt with His Pain, Your Gain or a hat with WWJD. It would have been hard to get someone to look me in the eye. Perhaps we need to think more deeply about what really makes for good evangelistic apparel.

You have influence! Your own example is often the best way to introduce the message of good news. Realizing that your life is not really your own will cause you to take advantage of the intersections God brings into your life. But God doesn't want you to feel like you're in a pressure cooker. Bringing people into God's kingdom is *his* work. It's not about your being a good salesman or having a slick presentation. Your part is simply being available as a tool in God's hands when you have the opportunity to connect people to grace and help them change the endings of their stories.

WHAT ABOUT YOU?

1. Have you ever had the opportunity to share the good news of Jesus with someone else? How did it go?

2. How would you answer the question "Why are you helping us?"

3. What one intersection has God specifically brought into your life in which you have the ability to influence someone else's story?

4. How can you bring the right amount of salt and light into the lives of others?

5. What are "common ground" activities you are already engaged in with your neighbors that God can use to further his purposes? How, specifically, do you see these as occasions for helping others change the course of their stories?

FORTUNE

Have you ever said "That guy's worth a fortune"? We think of fortune as a statement of wealth, but fortune is also a statement of God's providential blessing. The apostle James reminds us that "every good and perfect gift is from above, coming down from the Father" (James 1:17). The apostle Paul asks, "What do you have that you did not receive? And if you did receive it, why do you boast as though you did not?" (1 Corinthians 4:7). We are stewards, and not really owners, of all that God has given us. Fortune is a gift on loan from him.

But fortune also represents potential for the future. When we understand that God has trusted us as managers, we realize that managing our fortunes wisely has the potential of accomplishing great things. Dr. Henry Cloud exhorts us, "One of the worst things you can die with is potential. Die with failures before you die with potential."[1]

How can you take all the resources you have been given—your money, talents, and opportunities—and leverage them to expand the kingdom of God? You may not have much "fortune," but God can take the little you do have and use it to reach its full potential—for his glory.

6

LOVE GOD, LOVE YOUR NEIGHBOR

I must take care, on the one hand, never to despise, or be unthankful for,

these earthly blessings, and on the other, never to mistake them

for the something else of which they are only a kind of copy,

or echo, or mirage. I must keep alive in myself the desire for my true

country, which I shall not find till after death; I must never let it get

snowed under or turned aside; I must make it the main object of life to

press on to that other country and to help others to do the same.

—C. S. LEWIS

I (Rick) was with my family on a rare camping trip in upstate New York. (Our usual idea of roughing it was to stay at a Cheapskate Inn. But our two sons were in elementary school, and they loved the idea of camping out.) One afternoon we put a kite together. The blue sky and slight wind made it an ideal day to fly the kite. The boys were having a great time—both of them taking turns. They had the kite almost all the way out on the line when the string snapped and the kite went soaring into the distance—out of reach, gone, lost. It didn't take long to decide that we were going to go and find it. So I organized a focused, planned, and purposeful family search to find the kite.

I figured out in what direction we last saw our kite flying, guessed at how far the wind had taken the kite, and off we marched in pursuit of our kite. It wasn't long before our little search party was deep in the woods. It is true that the apple doesn't fall too far from the tree. My oldest son, David, was like me—focused, calculated, and determined to find that kite. But my son Eric and my wife were not much help. They were singing songs, looking under rocks, and exploring the forest. I will admit it was a bit irritating that they didn't seem as concerned about or focused on finding the kite as David and I were.

We managed to keep our two groups in sight of each other, but it had been some time since we were on the same path. It was especially irritating when Eric yelled out, "Look what we found!" *Of all the dumb luck,* David and I thought. *In their goofing around they've found the kite.* We made our way over to them. No kite—but there was a huge patch of wild blackberries fully in season. Juice dribbled down our cheeks and stained our shirts as we stuffed ourselves full of delicious blackberries. And right in the middle of our blackberry break, we could see something dangling in the branches of a tree about a hundred yards away. We had found our kite and continued to eat the blackberries. All in all, it was a good day.

What a wonderful find that patch of wild blackberries was! We went back to our campsite for some buckets and filled them with the blackberries, which we enjoyed for several days.

Life is rarely that clean or that simple. Tough situations, difficult relationships, and "lost kites" sometimes require all of our attention and energy. Have you sometimes missed the blackberries because you have been chasing kites? While David and I dutifully marched through the woods, Eric and Diane were enjoying the trip. My attitude reminds me of

Solomon's words, "So I hated life, because the work that is done under the sun was grievous to me. All of it is meaningless, a chasing after the wind" (Ecclesiastes 2:17).

How do you spend your time? What are your top priorities? What gets your attention, your energy, and your best? Every person is looking for his or her life to matter somehow. Jesus told a story about this very issue to make a point to an expert in the law—whom I like to think of as a Jewish attorney. Attorneys asking questions usually make people nervous. The Bible says that this particular expert in the law was asking less from sincerity and more as a test. He asked, "What must I do to inherit eternal life?" Jesus answered his question with a question, "What is written in the law? How do you read it?"

What are your top priorities? What gets your attention, your energy, and your best?

This was a tough question because not only were there the Ten Commandments Moses brought down from the mountain, but the Jewish law had over six hundred commandments that the religious leaders had defined, manipulated, and convoluted. It was tough to navigate.

What the expert was really asking was something like this: "So if I am going to see God, which of the commandments is the one I should pay most attention to?" He was asking whether there was a loophole around obeying all of them. Jesus asked, "Which do you think is the most important?" The attorney replied by reciting a verse from the book of Deuteronomy in the Old Testament, "'Love the Lord your God with all your heart and with all your soul and with all your strength and with all your mind'; and, 'Love your neighbor as yourself'" (Luke 10:27).

Jesus said that was a great answer and good choice, and if the attorney did that, he would get what he was asking for. Love God and love people. That pretty much sums it up. One important distinction that sets Christians apart from non-Christians who perform community service without a framework of faith in God is just that—our service to others is motivated by our love for God. In order to have a proper outward focus of helping people, we must first make sure the inward focus is right. Worship, teaching, and personal devotions are absolutely necessary for building the internal capacity necessary to sustain an external focus. It's much easier to meet people where they are at their place of need when we've already spent time meeting with our Father at our place of need.

In case there is any doubt that this man was an attorney, notice that he then asked Jesus for some clarification. In essence he was asking to see the fine print. He asked, "Who is my neighbor?" If the attorney was going to be a good neighbor, he needed to define whom he had to be good *to.* Was his neighbor just the person who lived next door, or his entire block? Would the people he passed on the way to work or at the grocery store technically be his neighbors? If he didn't know them, were they still his neighbors? "Who is my neighbor?"

It was in response to that question that Jesus told a story, the story of the Good Samaritan.

A GOOD NEIGHBOR

Even people who know little about the Bible or have never attended regular church services probably know a bit about this story. Someone was in trouble, and the Good Samaritan stopped to help (Luke 10:30-37). The victim in the story was beaten up, robbed of his stuff, and left for dead on the side of the road. Some people saw him but passed on by. But one person stopped to help him. In characteristic fashion, Jesus threw a twist into the story. The good guy in the story was a Samaritan. Jesus was telling his story to a Jewish man and, more than likely, in front of a Jewish crowd. Jews and Samaritans had a long-standing, deep hatred for each other. Their social and racial differences had become barriers long ago, and they took great pains to avoid each other.

The first guy to approach this beaten, left-for-dead, naked man lying on the side of the road was a priest, one of the religious leaders of the day. They were the guys who had cornered the market on God. What did the priest do when he saw the man? He crossed the street and kept right on going. The second man to see the beaten fellow was a teacher of the law—an expert. He also kept going on his merry way.

There was a time when I would hear this story and judge, "How selfish, how unloving, how unconscionable! Not to stop and help someone in need?" But the truth is, maybe I would have been like those guys who passed on by. Maybe they had planned on sending help back. Maybe they were concerned about getting mugged themselves. It's possible that this guy was just lying in wait to harm them. Maybe they prayed. Maybe they had important meetings to get to that took precedence over stopping to help just one person. It is possible that they were on their way to do some good things or maybe even better things. All Jesus shared with his listeners was that these two, the priest and the law expert, didn't stop.

Jesus says it was a third man—a Samaritan—who stopped to help. He saw a need and stopped to meet that need. It's simple and thoughtful. He could have crossed the street, ignored the problem, gone on his way . . . but he didn't. He got off his donkey and helped the man. It's possible he was just a do-gooder. Or maybe he was with the Looking for Half-Dead People Lying on the Side of the Road Agency, and he was just doing his job. It's more likely that he too had an agenda and a full plate, with things to do and people to see. It's not likely this Samaritan woke up that morning and said, "I sure hope that I can find some person lying on the road so I can stop to help him. That would really make my day!" Martin Luther King Jr. made this observation about the Good Samaritan: "The first question which the priest and the Levite asked was: 'If I stop to help this man, what will happen to me?' But . . . the good Samaritan reversed the question: 'If I do not stop to help this man, what will happen to him?'"[1]

Getting out of our own way is difficult, and going *out of our own way is even more difficult.*

This is one of those types of intersections God sends our way where, if we are paying attention, we might just see an opportunity. The Samaritan found himself at one of those moments when a life on loan makes a difference. Truth is, we often find a way around those moments, don't we? We have an opportunity to help, to stop and get off our donkey, but we find a way around it.

Your intersections may not involve an incident on the roadway; in fact, they usually involve the people right around you. It could be a person who looks discouraged, but you don't stop to encourage her. It could be a friend who calls and you sense something in his voice, but you don't take the time to ask "What's up?" Maybe it's the coworker who is struggling, the neighbor you ignore, the stranger you encounter, or your family or community with needs.

It isn't that we don't care or that we aren't good-hearted; we are just too busy. We have schedules, plans, agendas, and we have kites to chase. Getting out of our own way is difficult, and *going* out of our own way is even more difficult. So how did the Samaritan in Jesus' story become "good"? He recognized a need, got off his donkey, and took the time to meet the need.

He got his hands dirty

"He went to him and bandaged his wounds, pouring on oil and wine."

The Samaritan cleaned up the man and bandaged his wounds. This guy got his hands dirty. He wasn't just standing on the side of the road calling for help on his cell phone. If you are going to serve others, to live in God's grace, to offer your life as on loan for God's purposes, then it might get a bit messy. You might have to move outside your comfort zone. The people you meet along your life's journey aren't all going to have their acts together. You aren't going to be able to help others without getting your hands dirty.

He was inconvenienced

"Then he put the man on his own donkey."

He gave up his means of transportation and put the man on his donkey to take him for more help. When you choose to get involved, it is almost guaranteed that it isn't going to be at a convenient time. We often don't mind helping out when it is on our terms at our convenience. We sometimes limit our serving others to what fits into our daily planners. It's easier to give up something when we have planned for it, but sometimes our neighbors have needs that we haven't planned for.

He provided lodging and companionship

"He . . . took him to an inn and took care of him."

The Samaritan hung out with this guy for a while. Somehow he was able to see past the half-deadness and see a person. He didn't just see the man's predicament and how he might have gotten himself into that situation; he saw a real person, someone with a name and a story and a future. It took time to do that. Most of the time, people need connection more than they need anything else. The disenfranchised of the world need your humanity—relationship, friendship, respect, and regard—not just a passing thought of pity. Everyone has a name, everyone has a story, and everyone needs another person who knows that story.

He provided money

"The next day he took out two silver coins and gave them to the innkeeper. 'Look after him,' he said, 'and when I return, I will reimburse you for any extra expense you may have.'"

It's interesting that the last thing the Samaritan did was to provide money. It's usually easier to give money than to get involved. Writing a check or giving a handout salves our consciences and can ease the guilt we feel for others' circumstances. It enables us to help someone (money certainly does help) without becoming engaged in the person's life.

It takes money to meet the needs in your community or your neighborhood. You should give, but never at the expense of involvement. Keep finding ways to give, but don't substitute giving for compassion or for connection. If giving money is all you do, then you will miss out on what it means to be a good neighbor.

LOVING PEOPLE

Remember where we started on this journey of the Good Samaritan? Jesus was answering the "Who is my neighbor?" question from the expert in the law. So that there was no missing the point, Jesus asked him one final question, "Which one of these three do you think was a neighbor to the man who fell into the hands of robbers?" With no other option, the lawyer replied, "The one who had mercy on him."

Jesus said, "Go and do likewise" (Luke 10:36, 37). In other words, Jesus says to all of us, "Go and love people!"

It appears that the first step to being a good neighbor is to get off your donkey and do something. There are plenty of people in communities just like yours who have gotten off their donkeys and are making a difference. The Good Samaritan epitomizes the adage, "I am only one person. I cannot help everyone, but I can help someone. I cannot do everything, but I can do something." Who is your "someone"? What is your "something"? Let the following real stories inspire you to reassign, in your own unique way, your resources of time, talent, and treasure and to use your fortune to practically demonstrate love to people.

Appreciating fire station 3

The sacrifice of over three hundred firefighters who responded to the September 11, 2001 tragedy at the World Trade Center towers galvanized all Americans to set aside their differences and offer a united front of patriotism and gratitude.[2] As time went by, however, the heroism witnessed on that occasion seemed to be forgotten as petty differences and concerns once again crept back to the front stage of most people's lives—but not for Charity and Katie.

On the one-year anniversary of the 9/11 tragedy, these two young moms baked cookies for the fire and police stations around their own town. They wrote a personal note on each plate of cookies they dropped off. One year later, more neighbors and friends joined in as these two ladies organized a memorial dinner. Charity and Katie involved the whole community in this annual recognition as they contacted restaurants and businesses to request donations and gifts to benefit the fire stations across town. This part of the idea stemmed from the New York tradition of a firefighter's getting a free meal when he or she shows up in uniform at a local eatery.

"The response was overwhelming," Charity says. A local grocery store donated a cake, another one offered the decorations for the party, and restaurants and businesses gave certificates for free meals and gift baskets. "Some restaurant managers paid for these gifts themselves and many went a step further, sending thank-you cards signed by their employees along with the certificates," Katie adds.

Several families assisted Charity and Katie as they took care of each detail from planning to cleanup. "The only rule we had was that the food had to be home-cooked," explains Charity. "It had to come from the heart." Most firefighters who were on duty joined in the celebration, and some off-duty firemen brought their families to the event. The firefighters were amazed at how much Charity and Katie were able to accomplish.

"Everyone in the department got at least one gift certificate," Charity says. "We later found out some of the firefighters had wanted to save their certificates to donate them to other families in need." A few days later, the newspaper ran an advertisement paid for by the firefighters themselves, thanking the community for this show of support.

"We want our children to be raised watching how important it is to serve and appreciate others," Charity says. "You can show God's love without being 'preachy' by reaching out not just to your Christian friends but to your community." A simple project by two stay-at-home moms turned into a community-wide event of gratitude.

Remember to breathe

After forty years of smoking brought him face-to-face with emphysema, pneumonia, and other respiratory and heart issues, Bob knew he needed a change.[3] So he quit smoking and started a low-impact physical fitness program designed by his physical therapist. Results came quickly. But Bob didn't keep the good news to himself. He decided that if he could benefit from this life change, so could others. He rounded up a few other seniors and began a Chair-Aerobics fitness hour in the church activities center. Now he's the Richard Simmons of the senior citizens in his town and at his church.

Initially, only five people were showing up to march and swing their arms to the music, but today that group has grown to include more senior adults. They turn on 1940s big band music and begin stepping and stretching with Bob.

During the exercise routine, Bob shares short nuggets of wisdom such as "Many things are opened by mistake, but none so often as the mouth." He also interjects the taped instructions with, "Remember to breathe!" That's ironic, since the man leading the charge is attached to an oxygen tank twenty-four hours a day, seven days a week. Along with the leadership Bob provides in the exercise routine, he offers encouragement by sharing devotion times and personally caring for the members of the class.

"We want our children to be raised watching how important it is to serve and appreciate others."

Not only has Bob gathered the troops to exercise, he's taught them that their friendships are food for the soul as well. "I am going to wear out, not rust out," says one participant. Obviously Bob's determination is contagious. His only prerequisite for coming to the class is, "You must be breathing!"

Pilgrim62

Pilgrim62 is his World Wide Web e-mail address, but he doesn't leave West Virginia much.[4] He's not a world traveler or a corporate vice president. He doesn't shop at Nordstrom's or drive a large sport utility vehicle. He seems to be happy, but he didn't choose Happy62 as his e-mail address. He chose Pilgrim62 because he knows, first and foremost, that he's a pilgrim on a never-ending spiritual journey with marvelous twists and turns, hills and valleys.

Pilgrim62 delivers mail on a rural route in West Virginia. He drives a usually dirty Subaru with the steering column on the right-hand side so it's easier to deliver the mail to the rural mailboxes. On Sundays he preaches at a country church that has been around for generations. Pilgrim62 serves as a board member for a nonprofit corporation with people like himself and with others who aren't like him at all. At the meetings, he treats every individual as if he or she is the ambassador of an important foreign nation; Pilgrim62 believes that every person has dignity. He listens intently to each word spoken by every single person. For those who have developmental disabilities and have a difficult time speaking, he leans in close and gives voice to mouthed words.

Ask the typical American elementary school student what a pilgrim is, and he or she will tell you about the Pilgrims, that early seventeenth-century group of British Protestants who wanted to pursue religious freedom. Press a little further and you might hear "They wanted the freedom to pursue happiness." Those are words from our Declaration of Independence, but the Pilgrims seemed to understand it wasn't about happiness. That's a good thing because their experience in the New World wasn't abundantly happy. Their pilgrimage was a spiritual journey fraught with many struggles.

Without many words, Pilgrim62 reminds those around him to slow down, breathe a little easier, and talk about the ongoing pilgrimage we all share. Through his simple life and profound love for people, he reminds his fellow board members (with their Nordstrom jackets and cell phones) that we are all on a journey together and that every person deserves dignity, patience, and understanding.

Passing the love on

When we first met Kate about three years ago, she had come into the church office requesting financial assistance. At the time, we couldn't meet her need, and she yelled at our staff in frustration. Later we called her and said, "We can't pay your bill, but we can get you on the list to get some Christmas gifts for your two daughters." She was more thrilled that we actually called her back than she was with the idea of gifts.

Kate continued to ask occasionally for help in small ways. After several years of that on-again, off-again benevolence help, Kate and one of her daughters started coming to church. This daughter received a scholarship to go to camp, and Kate participated in the single moms program at the church. Now she works on the custodial crew, which is her night job. Every month is still a tremendous financial strain for her.

Kate recently approached the staff with a new request. A family she knew was in need of help. The father had lost his job due to an extended serious illness, and the mother had cancer. Kate said, "I don't know what to do, but I know I'm supposed to help these people. You know, I learned that my life is on loan, and I've got to make a difference." Kate is learning to give, to love, and to live beyond her own life and circumstances.

Taking time to care

Every morning Mike stopped at the same gas station to fill up. He wasn't interested in paying at the pump, though it would have been more convenient. He went in to pay, often picking up a Diet Coke and a candy bar and joking with the station attendant, saying, "Sure hope this Diet Coke cancels out the calories in the candy bar." One morning as he laughed with the attendant, he noticed "Melissa" on her name tag, and from then on, he greeted her by name.

Even if the gas gauge wasn't sitting on empty, Mike stopped by and went in. And even though gas was sometimes cheaper at the station across the street, he continued to stop by Melissa's station. Over time Mike came to learn that Melissa was a single mother.

During their brief encounters each morning, Mike occasionally mentioned something happening at his church. After some time, Melissa was invited to attend a wedding at Mike's church. "After the wedding I caught up with Melissa and once again invited her to come back on a Sunday," says Mike. A few weeks after that invitation, Melissa finally visited Mike's church. Within one month, she asked to meet with him to learn more about Jesus.

Mike is one of those individuals who loves people, not simply giving money or serving with projects, but by following the example of Jesus when he resisted the urge to hurry to something more important. In Luke 8, we see a woman in a crowd touch Jesus because she wanted to be healed. Jesus resisted the temptation to hurry along and ignore her need, even though it was not a convenient time for him to stop; he was on his way to heal a little girl whose father was a leader in the synagogue. "As Jesus was on his way, the crowds almost crushed him. And a woman was there who had been subject to bleeding for twelve years, but no one could heal her. She came up behind him and touched the edge of his cloak, and immediately her bleeding stopped" (Luke 8:42-44). The woman was instantly healed.

Jesus didn't have to stop, but he chose to. Jesus took time for her even as the crowd was crushing him. I'm sure that the woman who was healed was thankful that Jesus slowed down enough to heal her, and I'm sure that Melissa is grateful Mike thought twice before paying at the pump.

Loving older people

Cee is an active senior adult and involved in many things. Long ago she made the decision to serve others even when it wasn't the most enjoyable thing she could be doing. Cee has chosen to adopt some of the older individuals in her community who, for one reason or another, are pretty much on their own. She takes them out to eat and to doctors' appointments. She delivers their favorite snacks, visits with them, and gets them out doing things if they are able.

Cee has made a conscious choice to be engaged in their lives even when it hasn't been easy to do so. Recently she said, "Service may bring sorrow or joy to you. It won't always be easy. But most of all it will provide purpose and direction to your life as you follow Jesus."

Ransoming the slaves

When I (Eric) was in China in 2003, I met a young woman I'll call Stacy. Stacy came to Christ at the age of nineteen and almost immediately felt God calling her to China. So she moved to Hong Kong for a couple of years where she worked with street kids and learned Cantonese—the language of southern China. But her heart was still restless; she felt that God was asking her to move into a large city in mainland China.

For safety and security issues, we can't disclose the city, but we can tell you Stacy's story. She moved to this large city, unsure of her mission or ministry. As she was now learning Mandarin, the language of most of China, she began to meet children who were street beggars, and she took them to a Western fast-food restaurant for burgers. Little by little the stories of these children unfolded.

Stacy explains that in rural areas there are some villages that are so poor there is literally no money—let alone jobs; that leaves these people hope-starved and vulnerable. Men known as "bosses," from large cities often hundreds of miles away, come to these villages offering to pay the parents twenty dollars per month to take their children to the city where they will supposedly receive education and job training. I know this sounds like something from a medieval fairy tale or a Charles Dickens story, but these kids are then taken to the cities and forced to beg, sell flowers, or wash windshields. They live in a cramped hovel without toilets or running water. If they do not earn enough money to meet their daily quota for their bosses, they are beaten.

Stacy's heart melted, and she fell in love with these street kids. She threw birthday parties for them, took them sightseeing, and took them to restaurants to teach them manners. But she wanted to do more.

Today Stacy is twenty-nine years old and has forty children living with her in a larger home. Nearly all of the children have become followers of Jesus.

Since most of the children were from rural provinces, she had to travel several hundred miles to meet with the parents of these children. In most instances, it was the first time a Westerner had visited the villages. Stacy told the parents the truth about what was happening, but then she did something more. Stacy offered to pay the parents twenty dollars a month to have the children live with *her,* where they really would be educated and cared for. She was buying out the street bosses' contracts, ransoming the slaves, setting the captives free.

At the time I visited Stacy's home, she had twenty-five young teens living with her. They were well dressed and groomed, with impeccable manners. Her home is about what she calls "re-parenting" and "re-loving" these children. Stacy says, "How much love they receive determines how much love they have to give." The children's days consist of Bible study, corporate worship, English classes, computer classes, recreation, and household chores. Three nights a week they go back on the street and talk with other street children.

Today Stacy is twenty-nine years old and has forty children living with her in a larger home. Nearly all of the children have become followers of Jesus. Stacy's story continues to intersect with the stories of others. And their stories are becoming God's story in China.

These are just a few stories that illustrate what can happen when people take seriously Jesus' challenge to love God and love their neighbors. It causes them to reprioritize their lives and reassign their resources—whether that's time, talents, or treasure. People who are living their lives as if on loan are writing similar stories every day. Every single day we add another page to our stories. What story are you writing? Whose life are you intersecting? Your actions can make a lasting difference.

WHAT ABOUT YOU?

1. Can you recall a time when you lost focus on what really matters in your life?

2. How does that kind of lost focus occur?

3. Note a time when you have been a "Good Samaritan."

4. How did that make you feel?

5. What is one priority on your list whose place you need to shift? What is one resource whose use you need to rethink?

7

INVESTING BIG
AND LITTLE RESOURCES

Life is not a journey to the grave with the intention of arriving

safely in a pretty and well preserved body,

but rather to skid in sideways, thoroughly used up, totally

worn out, and loudly proclaiming "Wow—what a ride!"

—PETER SAGE

Archimedes was born in Sicily in the year 287 BC. He was a brilliant mathematician, physicist, and inventor who used his inventions of pulleys and catapults to help the Greeks prevail in battle—and he used his equation for finding the radius of a sphere to stump geometry students throughout the ages! He is credited with saying, "Give me a lever long enough and a fulcrum on which to place it, and I shall move the world."[1] Archimedes understood the power of leverage—how something relatively small (a lever and a fulcrum) can be used to move something very, very large. He understood that if the lever is long enough and the fulcrum is strong enough, the rest is just a matter of physics.

Unfortunately for Archimedes and his idea of moving the world, there was no such lever and no such fulcrum. But that doesn't diminish the principle of leverage. Small things you do can make a huge difference.

Just as most people know the story of the Good Samaritan, the Twenty-third Psalm is equally well known. It is a section of the Bible most often read at funerals—even funerals for nonreligious people. In Psalm 23, David penned some of the most comforting words ever written—words of green pastures, quiet waters, and peace amid much danger in "the valley of the shadow of death" (v. 4). But in a lesser-known psalm, Psalm 24, David explained why he could have such peace. David writes, "The earth is the LORD's, and everything in it, the world, and all who live in it" (Psalm 24:1).

David had figured out something that few people discover—it all belongs to God. "Everything" is all-inclusive. "All" includes everybody! That means even though you feel like you are the owner of your resources, it is really God who is the owner. Then what does that make *you?* Well, you are a steward, a manager, of everything God has entrusted to you. Everything you have is on loan from God. If that's true, then how does God want you to invest your resources?

A LITTLE GOES A LONG WAY

If your life and your stuff are on loan from God, what can you do to make the most of it all? The great news is that you don't need much to leverage in order to make a large impact, partly because God measures things a bit differently than we do. When Jesus and his disciples were observing people as they put their offerings in the collection box at the temple, Jesus showed us just what kind of scale God uses. The story reads like this:

Jesus sat down opposite the place where the offerings were put and watched the crowd putting their money into the temple treasury. Many rich people threw in large amounts. But a poor widow came and put in two very small copper coins, worth only a fraction of a penny. Calling his disciples to him, Jesus said, "I tell you the truth, this poor widow has put more into the treasury than all the others. They all gave out of their wealth; but she, out of her poverty, put in everything—all she had to live on (Mark 12:41-44).

Jesus says the paltry offering of the widow added up to more than anyone else's gift and perhaps more than all of them put together! It wasn't the greatness of the gift Jesus was talking about but the greatness of the response of this dear woman. Even though her resources were few, she leveraged what she had by putting everything into God's hands. Sometimes your greatest leverage begins simply with *wanting* to accomplish something more.

There's another biblical account about investing little to accomplish much. People had been following Jesus. Captivated by his teachings and miracles, they'd neglected to take any food along. The disciples urged Jesus to send the crowds away so they could go buy food, but Jesus responded, "They do not need to go away. You give them something to eat" (Matthew 14:16). Without enough food on hand, the disciples had a dilemma. They could insist on sending the crowd away—then everyone could eat but not be with Jesus. Or they could stay put—listening to thousands of stomachs growl.

Jesus had another option—they could stay with him *and* eat and be satisfied. The miraculous solution came through a boy who'd had the foresight to bring bread and some small fish. A few pieces of bread and fish didn't seem like much to put into the hands of Jesus. In fact, one disciple remarked, "How far will they go among so many?" (John 6:9).

But those familiar with the story will recall that everyone was fed—and there were twelve basketfuls of leftovers.

There's an old movie called *The Inn of the Sixth Happiness,* starring Ingrid Bergman. It is the true-to-life account of Gladys Aylward who, as a young girl, dreamed of being a missionary to China. After three months of missionary training school, the mission society broke the news to her—she was not qualified to serve in China. Undeterred, she saved her meager wages as a housekeeper and took the Trans-Siberian train across Europe, Russia, and eventually China, where she joined an aging woman who strategically set up an inn for muleteers.

When we make the most of our resources without expecting recognition or reward, great things happen—and God gets the glory.

Gladys, disqualified by man but approved and qualified by God, made the most of all she had, leading many Chinese people to Christ and taking one hundred orphaned children one hundred miles to safety when Japan attacked China in the 1930s. At the end of her life, Gladys wrote of herself, "My heart is full of praise that one so insignificant, uneducated, and ordinary in every way could be used to His glory for the blessing of His people in poor persecuted China."[2] That's the power of leverage in a life on loan.

Sometimes others look at our unremarkable abilities (as they looked at Gladys) or at our limited resources (as they looked at the boy with his bread and fish) and remark, "Well, what could you ever do?" But put bread and fish into the hands of Jesus, and he multiplies that to feed five thousand people . . . with plenty to spare. Availability seems to be of greater consequence than ability alone.

It's interesting to note that the boy with the bread and fish has never been identified by name . . . and that's probably how it should be. When we make the most of our resources without expecting recognition or reward, great things happen—and God gets the glory. At the end of the story, we find the people applauding Jesus, not the boy (see John 6:14).

THE EIGHT TALENTS

Perhaps the best Bible story on leveraging resources comes from Jesus when he was teaching his friends about the kingdom of God. Jesus told them the kingdom of God is "like a man going on a journey, who called his servants and entrusted his property to them. To one he gave five talents of money, to another two talents, and to another one talent, each according to his ability" (Matthew 25:14, 15).

The gist of the story

The master represents Jesus—the one who was preparing to go away. We are his servants. A talent in Jesus' day was a large amount of money—about a thousand dollars. And when you consider the average wage for a soldier or laborer in Bible times was a silver denarius (a mere seventeen cents per day), a thousand dollars was a whole lot of money.

It appears that the master entrusted *all* his money to his servants and left the outcome in their hands. He didn't have a Plan B. He didn't give the money to professional investors but rather to his servants. These talents were truly on loan from God, which meant the servants were not owners of the money but were stewards. Note also that each was entrusted with an amount of money that corresponded to individual abilities. One of the servants was given nearly twice what the remaining two servants received together.

How many "talents" has God given to you? Perhaps you have been entrusted with much. On the other hand, perhaps you have been entrusted with very little. Maybe you just have your daily wage of seventeen cents! In any case, you have the potential to impact the kingdom of God in a great way.

As we read the rest of the story, we find out that the first two servants were geared toward action. They immediately put the money to work for the master and secured a 100-percent return. And even though the quantity of the money they returned to the master was unequal, the praise and commendation they received was the same (Matthew 25:21, 23). The servant who received just one talent, a thousand dollars, was afraid of losing it, so he buried it. He played it safe. When the master returned, he rewarded the two servants who had doubled their money, but he severely chastised the one who gave the original investment back. The master assigned him to a place of darkness, tears, and pain.

> *We need to be using our resources wisely until Jesus comes back.*

The trouble with the story

The truth is, I (Rick) don't really like this story. If I were telling the story, I would have distributed the talents equally so each would have received 2.666666 talents. After all, things should be fair. If I couldn't give them equal talents, I would have told the story with the five-talent guy losing and the one-talent man succeeding. (Who doesn't want to root for the underdog?) I also don't like this story because the master doesn't seem to be a very reasonable person. He gives unequal amounts, doesn't leave specific instructions for the money, shows up unexpectedly, and wants an account of what was done.

I just don't like this story, but it isn't my story. It is a story that Jesus told right after he was asked when he would be coming back. Instead of answering the question with a specific date or time, Jesus told stories, and one of those was this story about investments. So the message is that we need to be using our resources wisely until Jesus comes back.

Why did the one-talent man in Jesus' story fail?

He thought easier was better

He decided that he could keep the money safe if he hid it in his backyard, so he dug a hole and buried the treasure. I don't really know what his neighborhood was like, but I can't help imagining that he took the money, went home and got a shovel out of the garage, made sure the neighbors weren't watching, and buried the talent. After that he could just coast because the money was safe. There would be no losing that talent . . . it was right where he could keep his eye on it. But was this really easier? Now he would have to get a guard dog and a motion detector light for his backyard. He might have to purchase a metal detector so he could go out every evening and make sure that the money was still in the hole. He probably woke at the slightest of noises to see who might be stealing what he had buried. Maybe he found out that it really was a lot of work to keep his talent safe.

He was just plain lazy

The servant hid the talent, and that required little effort. He didn't do anything with what he had been given. When the master returned, the servant only had to blow the dust off the money and bring it back just as it had been given to him. He returned all of the talent but still is called lazy and wicked.

He played it too safe

Sure, it's good that he didn't invest the money in a crazy scheme or gamble it away or lose it. But he didn't look for any way at all to multiply the money for his master. The talent remained safe in his own backyard—intact . . . and unused. For this, he got tossed into outer darkness where there is "weeping and gnashing of teeth" (v. 30). Whatever that means, it doesn't sound too good. What if this one-talent man had tried, taken a reasonable risk, or found a way to use what he had been given? His failure was that he did nothing. He didn't even make an attempt. I saw on a T-shirt the quote that opens this chapter. It really sums up what it means to make a great attempt at living your life outside of the safety zone: "Life is not a journey to the grave with the intention of arriving safely in a pretty and well preserved body, but rather to skid in sideways, thoroughly used up, totally worn out, and proclaiming 'Wow—what a ride!'"

The point of the story

The implication of Jesus' story of the one-talent man is that we have each been given something of value. There is an expectation that it will be used for good and that someday the master will show up. Then we will give an accounting for what we have done with what was entrusted to us.

Maybe you have been unwilling to make the most of your resources. Perhaps you have felt unable in some ways. Maybe you didn't realize that you *had* resources. No matter. Your story isn't over yet. God is a God of second and third and one-hundredth chances. You may have found yourself in a dark place, but if you look, the light of God is there, available to bring you out of the darkness. All of us have the opportunity to get back up and into the game. We can somehow find ways to use for good our past, our heartache, our disappointment, our lack of trying, our playing safe, and our mistakes. God can use (and multiply!) our resources, no matter how unlikely or limited they seem.

ALL IN!

Our resources, many or few, can be leveraged into great things for God. But once we get a taste for seeing what God can accomplish through our willingness, we may want to invest even more.

Televised poker championships seem to be the current rage. Thanks to the invention of poker cams (miniature cameras that allow the television audience to see the players' concealed cards), the audience can follow every player's strategy. But the moment that captures every viewer's attention is when a player declares "All in!" and pushes his or her chips (often amounting to hundreds of thousands of dollars) to the center of the table.

The widow tossed in her last coins and declared, "All in!" The boy shoved his bread and fish to the center and said, "All in!" Gladys pushed her life to the center and announced, "All in!" Have you ever pushed your life from your side of the table into the center—into God's hands? You can. You can say "All in!" as others have done. That's when the adventure really takes off!

Lake Avenue Church in Pasadena, California, has a significant ministry to day laborers. Day laborers at the very bottom of the labor ladder may be somewhat of a California phenomenon. They receive no benefits and hold no permanent position, but are hired (or not hired) on a day-to-day basis and paid an hourly wage. Often undocumented, day laborers are part of the "don't ask, don't tell" segment of the American economy. The agriculture and service sectors of our economy depend on them, but at the same time there is growing movement to get rid of them. What resources could a day laborer use to help others?

Because day laborers are made in the image of God like everybody else, they too have a desire for their lives to count. So a group of day laborers came up with the idea of helping to prepare and serve meals to the homeless every Sunday night at Lake Avenue Church!

The laborers made the most of the little they had to serve and minister to those who had even less. What could you do with the little you have?

Several years ago I (Eric) was in Calcutta, India, visiting Mother Teresa's Missionaries of Charity. Mother Teresa cast her lot with the outcasts of the world, the poorest of the poor, and people with leprosy, blindness, and crippling diseases—those rejected by family and society.

Mother Teresa is not admired for any one big thing in her life that stands out, but she is admired for a series of small things done consistently over time.

We visited two of her homes that day. The first was *Shishu Bhavan* (Home for Babies)—which housed children who were orphans or had been abandoned. Holding and playing with these precious children was very enjoyable. Then we went to *Nirmal Hriday* (Home for the Destitute and Dying)—a place for men and women who had been found on the streets at death's door and had been bathed, dressed, and given a home where they would be loved and cared for until they died.

Here were two radically different experiences with people at the opposite ends of life's spectrum, but the care and the love at the two homes is consistent. Mother Teresa has often said that "if she hadn't picked up the first person many years ago, the 77,500 plus wouldn't have been picked up off the streets."[3] Mother Teresa is not admired for any one big thing in her life that stands out, but she is admired for a series of small things done consistently over time—none that are beyond the skill level or reach of any average follower of Christ. In other words, one way to make the most of what you have is simply by doing small things over time.

A LIFE ON LOAN

Most likely, you have at some time taken out a loan and then had to pay back more than you borrowed. On the surface that may seem somewhat foolish, but if you prudently used the loan, it may have been a pretty good deal.

Accountants, business people, and debt counselors talk about two types of debt—good debt and bad debt. Good debt is money you borrow to acquire assets that appreciate. That is, you have more assets after the debt is paid off. First-home mortgages generally fall into this category. In certain cases, educational loans fall under good debt. Bad debt usually refers to loans you have taken out on depreciating or depleting assets. So plunking your VISA card down to buy the usual super-size Triple Whopper with cheese plus a chocolate shake and then not paying off the balance is probably a picture of bad debt (unless you consider your waistline an appreciating asset). A good loan benefits the lender with interest and the borrower with the benefits gained.

Since your life belongs to someone else and is on loan to you, there should be benefits for both the lender (God) and the borrower (you). Here's a helpful acrostic with each letter of the word *loan*. Each of the four terms gives us a few hints about what it means to live a life on loan.

Leverage

Sometimes you take out a loan as leverage. Leverage lets you get the biggest return for the least investment. Sometimes those who understand the stock market buy shares of publicly traded companies "on margin"— borrowed money—with the expectancy that the stock will appreciate. That is leverage. Understanding that your life is on loan will propel you to begin looking for ways to leverage your life—getting a thirty-, sixty-, and a hundred-times return on the life you have been loaned (see Matthew 13:23).

Opportunity

Sometimes you take out a loan to take advantage of a new opportunity. I (Rick) remember the first time I needed a loan to buy a house. Having just recently graduated from college and begun a new job, I did not have a whole lot of financial strength. The loan officer at the bank was a very polite woman who was patient enough to listen to me tell her about the house. While I didn't possess all the things she would have liked to see on my balance sheet, she too saw the opportunity and found a way to help me secure enough money to purchase the home. That bank certainly didn't loan me the money without some hope of its being paid back. They did, however, choose to make an investment in me that enabled me to invest in this new home. When we live a life on loan, we will look for opportunities and go after them.

Advance

Do you ever need an "advance" from God . . . when your responsibilities and obligations are much greater than your assets and abilities? Are you ever in way over your head? How many times have you felt like you are going under, and—to put it in financial terms—all of your checks are going to come back marked "insufficient funds" . . . and then God mercifully advances his grace toward you? If you don't think your life is on loan—if you think you can manage just fine on your own—try living without his overdraft protection!

Need

Have you ever been so broke that you needed a loan just to get by? Chances are you went to a sympathetic friend to ask for help. If that friend had the resources, you probably got what you needed.

Perhaps the word *need* describes most clearly something we really must understand about living a life on loan. You have so much to do, so few resources to do it with, and a limited time in which to do it. This state of continual neediness draws you back in prayer to God, your sympathetic friend . . . and he gives you what you need today. The Bible says, "Do not withhold good from those who deserve it, when it is in your power to act. Do not say to your neighbor, 'Come back later; I'll give it tomorrow'—when you now have it with you" (Proverbs 3:27). God does not withhold. Acknowledging that God is the owner and you are simply the manager keeps you coming back to him for what you need.

INVEST WHAT YOU'VE GOT

Jesus not only commended people who leveraged what they had, but he also taught about it—about accomplishing something very great with something very small. The closest disciples of Jesus were having trouble doing something he had asked them to do. When they came to Jesus and asked why they couldn't do it, he referred to their lack of faith. "I tell you the truth, if you have faith as small as a mustard seed, you can say to this mountain, 'Move from here to there' and it will move. Nothing will be impossible for you" (Matthew 17:20).

Faith is that elusive lever that can move the world. (Someone really should have told Archimedes!) Combining your resources with faith—the faith that God will take what you have and use it—shows a major step in understanding leverage. It's not the size of your resources but rather the size of your God that really makes the difference. God can do in a moment what it might take men a lifetime to achieve.

Most material things, unless they are explicitly spoken against in the Bible, are pretty much morally neutral. By themselves they cause neither help nor harm. But with every possession comes a pressure to care for that possession or make sure you use it enough to make owning it worth the cost. You may know people who rush off every weekend to their cabin simply because they feel they must use it to justify what they paid for it—even after they've discovered that they really don't care for the mountains or lakeside living. In such a case, the possession (the cabin) isn't really being used well. It isn't accomplishing all it could. The owners need to rethink how to make the most of what they have.

Each of us has been entrusted with things that can be used to accomplish God's purposes—time, our own bodies, and our money and possessions.

Invest your time

There are two types of time mentioned in the Bible—chronological time (as in the passing of days, weeks, months, and years) and time as opportune moments. You have been entrusted with a set number of days on earth. Psalm 139 says, "All the days ordained for me were written in your book before one of them came to be" (v. 16). This is chronological time. We've all been given twenty-four hours in a day, one hundred sixty-eight hours in a week, and approximately seventy years to live. That's a lot of time in which to accomplish good. On the other hand, the Bible also reminds us, "Be careful how you walk, not as unwise men, but as wise, making the most of your time" (Ephesians 5:15, 16, *NASB*).

We'll say more about time and eternity in later chapters, but the word used for "time" in this way means "opportunity" rather than chronological time. There are opportune moments—windows of opportunity—that you need to take advantage of if you want to fulfill the purpose God has given to you. What does God want you to do with your time? He wants you to make the most of it.

Invest your body

Writing to believers in Corinth, Paul said, "Do you not know that your body is a temple of the Holy Spirit, who is in you, whom you have received from God? You are not your own; you were bought at a price. Therefore honor

God with your body" (1 Corinthians 6:19, 20). How can you honor God with your body? Paul has a couple of suggestions. He writes, "I urge you, brothers, in view of God's mercy, to offer your bodies as living sacrifices, holy and pleasing to God" (Romans 12:1). What does God want you to do with your body? Present it to him and keep it fit for his service.

God gives everyone only one body to last a lifetime. Robert Mc-Cheyne was a minisiter in Scotland in the 1800s. He worked tirelessly. Just before his premature death at the youthful age of twenty-nine, he wrote, "God gave me a message to deliver and a horse to ride. Alas, I have killed the horse and now I cannot deliver the message."[4]

The late Dr. George Sheehan, who took up running at age forty-five and wrote several books on running and fitness, often said, "Don't be concerned if running or exercise will add years to your life; be concerned with adding life to your years."[5] Though his statement seems to emphasize life purpose over physical fitness, he did point out that people who are physically fit have energy to start their second day when they get off work. In this sense, an hour of daily exercise can be leveraged into eight hours of renewed productivity to enhance relationships, serve others, and engage in ministry.

Choosing an exercise you enjoy is a great way to keep your body in shape. The late Pope John Paul II was more than likely the most athletic pope. As a youth he was an avid sportsman—playing hockey, soccer, and enjoying swimming, hiking, and skiing. For the first fifteen years of his papacy, he took an annual ski vacation. In 1979 he had a swimming pool built at the papal summer residence. At a press conference, one reporter asked John Paul how he could account for allocating funds to build a swimming pool at the papal summer palace in view of all the needs of the world. He candidly responded, "I like to swim. Next question."[6] He understood the need for restorative exercise and recreation in order to be more productive.

Invest your money and possessions

In Paul's first letter to his friend and coworker Timothy, he outlined instructions regarding values and behavior for different groups of people in the church—men, women, children, and widows. Among these instructions were some guidelines for those who are rich:

> Command those who are rich in this present world not to be arrogant nor to put their hope in wealth, which is so uncertain, but to put their hope in God, who richly provides us with everything for our enjoyment. Command them to do good, to be rich in good deeds, and to be generous and willing to share. In this way they will lay up treasure for themselves as a firm foundation for the coming age, so that they may take hold of the life that is truly life (1 Timothy 6:17-19).

His instructions speak to us today.

Don't be arrogant. Don't assume you have wealth because you are so talented and smart. As the saying goes, "If you see a turtle on a fencepost, you know it didn't get there by itself."

Take hold of the life that is truly life.

Don't put your hope in wealth. Instead, put your hope in God.

Do good! Be rich in good deeds. Money is a great tool but a poor master.

Be generous and willing to share—enough said!

It is interesting that Paul also says that if you do this, you will "take hold of the life that is truly life." Isn't that a great expression—life that is truly life? Mother Teresa wrote, "I think that a person who is attached to riches, who lives with the worry of riches, is actually very poor. However, if such a person puts her money at the service of others, then she is rich, very rich."[7] What does God want you to do with your money and possessions? He wants you to leverage them to accomplish his purposes. How can you do that?

There is a marvelous account in Luke that answers the question. In this passage, Jesus stops to interact with a man who has just intersected his message midstream.

> Someone in the crowd said to him, "Teacher, tell my brother to divide the inheritance with me." Jesus replied, "Man, who appointed me a judge or an arbiter between you?" Then he said to them, "Watch out! Be on your guard against all kinds of greed; a man's life does not consist in the abundance of his possessions." And he told them this parable: "The ground of a certain rich man produced a good crop. He thought to himself, 'What shall I do? I have no place to store my crops.' Then he said, 'This is what I'll do. I will tear down my barns and build bigger ones, and there I will store all my grain and my goods. And I'll say to myself, "You have plenty of good things laid up for many years. Take life easy; eat, drink and be merry."' But God said to him, 'You fool! This very night your life will be demanded from you. Then who will get what you have prepared for yourself?' This is how it will be with anyone who stores up things for himself but is not rich toward God" (Luke 12:13-21).

Did you notice the preponderance of self?—"myself," "my barns," "my crops," "my goods" . . . my yada, yada, yada! This man did not realize it was all on loan from God. Possessions should never be hoarded, but like other resources, they should be prioritized and used to accomplish God's purposes.

The leverage of giving is very simple. Paul writes, "Whoever sows sparingly will also reap sparingly, and whoever sows generously will also reap generously" (2 Corinthians 9:6). Planting seeds is always a leveraged activity. Small seeds produce big fruits and vegetables. And the more you sow, the more you will reap.

GIVING FROM THE HEART

Jesus suggested that you put your money where you want your heart to be. He said, "For where your treasure is, there your heart will be also" (Matthew 6:21). In other words, if you want your heart to be invested in something, put part of your treasure there. It's so easy to reverse this principle and think, *Well, when I get a heart for this, I'll invest some of my money there.* But it's the other way around. If you have ever bought a share of stock either on the New York Stock Exchange or the NASDAQ, you'll understand this principle. After you buy the stock, you get online every day just to see whether the stock has gone up or down. Because you led with your money, your heart followed. "Where your treasure is, there your heart will be also."

Several years ago a couple of friends of mine saw a slide show at their church, sponsored by a large organization that connects sponsors with children all over the world. Pete and Ann began investing a little bit of their treasure in the life of one girl from Thailand. Regularly they received letters from their child, and their hearts became more and more drawn into Thailand and the life of this small child—so much so that in 2000, the family took a trip to Thailand to visit their sponsored child. It was a wonderful time of bonding.

They had led with their treasure and ended up investing their hearts. Shortly after their visit, Pete resigned from his tech job and took a job with this charitable organization! What began with their treasure captured their hearts and eventually encompassed their lives. My friend Bob Horner likes to say, "The best way to invest your treasure in Heaven is by investing it in people who are going there."

Leveraging your financial resources is part of the path to spiritual maturity. Paul wrote to new followers of Christ, "Just as you excel in everything—in faith, in speech, in knowledge, in complete earnestness and in your love for us—see that you also excel in this grace of giving" (2 Corinthians 8:7). The process is not complete until you let the grace of God give you this grace of giving.

It's so easy to reverse this principle and think, Well, when I get a heart for this, I'll invest some of my money there. *But it's the other way around.*

Preachers like to remind us, "The last part of a man to be converted is his pocketbook."[8] Many of the soldiers of the Middle Ages were baptized while holding their swords. But the arm holding the sword was held above the water during the baptism. Apparently, the soldiers were unable to submit the sword to Jesus' lordship. Mentally we often do the same with our checkbooks. But if generosity is a hallmark of spiritual maturity, then a look inside our checkbooks will say a lot about our own spiritual maturity.

So what can you give to? How? And when? These days, there is much written about the subject of giving, largely because the Bible talks a lot about it. Here are a few guidelines regarding giving away your resources.

Give from the top

The Bible says, "Honor the LORD with your wealth, with the firstfruits of all your crops; then your barns will be filled to overflowing, and your vats will brim over with new wine" (Proverbs 3:9, 10).

Giving off the top creates the opportunity for God to fill in the gaps, either by increasing your income or reducing your outgo and expenses.

Tithing is not like tipping; tithing always comes from the firstfruits, but tipping comes from what you have left over. God is looking for people to be conduits of his grace. It makes great spiritual sense that as you faithfully use your financial resources to expand the kingdom of God, he will keep entrusting you with the resources to do so.

Give generously and proportionately

Peter Marshall, chaplain to the U.S. Senate in the late 1940s, reportedly once prayed, "Lord, let me give in proportion to my blessing lest you bless me in proportion to my giving."[9] Our generosity is a reflection of God's own dominant attribute of generosity. He is generous in love, grace, and mercy. Everything he does, he does with generosity. Our generosity begins with a willing attitude. Paul writes, "If the willingness is there, the gift is acceptable according to what one has, not according to what he does not have" (2 Corinthians 8:12).

Generosity is the opposite of hoarding. Loving money and stashing it is a dead-end game. Over twenty-five hundred years ago, King Solomon wrote, "Whoever loves money never has money enough; whoever loves wealth is never satisfied with his income" (Ecclesiastes 5:10). Mother Teresa once said, "I fear just one thing: money! Greed—the love of money—was what motivated Judas to sell Jesus."[10]

Give joyously

The Bible says, "Each man should give what he has decided in his heart to give, not reluctantly or under compulsion, for God loves a cheerful giver" (2 Corinthians 9:7). Do you dread going to events where eventually "The Sermon on the Amount" comes up? Being a generous giver doesn't mean that every need you learn of becomes your call to give. But it does create an openness to pray, "God, is this something you want me to partner with you in?"

If you give grudgingly, it's probably because you think you are parting with something that rightfully belongs to you. Mother Teresa came across a small family that was starving to death—literally. When she delivered food, the woman immediately cut the portion in half and took half to her neighbor! She joyously realized she was the conduit of God's grace to her neighbor.

Give to the needy

God gives his people the responsibility and privilege of mirroring his compassion and mercy. The Bible says, "He who is kind to the poor lends to the LORD, and he will reward him for what he has done" (Proverbs 19:17). It is said that half of all people in the world each live on only two dollars a day. With that in mind, think about the turtle on the fencepost. You didn't get where you are on your own. God has blessed you! How you treat the marginalized through your giving is an indicator of your relationship with God. Jesus talked frequently of giving. In one of his final teachings before his crucifixion, Jesus said,

> "I was hungry and you gave me something to eat, I was thirsty and you gave me something to drink, I was a stranger and you invited me in, I needed clothes and you clothed me, I was sick and you looked after me, I was in prison and you came to visit me." Then the righteous will answer him, "Lord, when did we see you hungry and feed you, or thirsty and give you something to drink? When did we see you a stranger and invite you in, or needing clothes and clothe you? When did we see you sick or in prison and go to visit you?" The King will reply, "I tell you the truth, whatever you did for one of the least of these brothers of mine, you did for me" (Matthew 25:35-40).

John the Baptist, the guy who wore camel's hair and ate locusts and wild honey, was Jesus' cousin. He had a powerful message. When John the

Baptist started his ministry, part of his message on the kingdom of God included producing "fruit in keeping with repentance" (Luke 3:8). When people in the crowd asked specifically what they were to do, the first thing John mentioned pertained to generosity toward others: "The man with two tunics should share with him who has none, and the one who has food should do the same" (Luke 3:11).

Here's a practical suggestion: the next time you buy a car, instead of trying to get top dollar for your trade-in, why not donate it to a single mom to help with her transportation needs?

Give to help expand the kingdom of God

The Bible says, "God blesses us, that all the ends of the earth may fear Him" (Psalm 67:7, *NASB*). Somehow God's blessing to you must be reinvested in people so they will come to know him. There are several opportunities to sponsor individuals, strategies, and organizations that bring the good news to those you can never get to. You can also support individuals and organizations that plant churches.

Remember to give to those who minister to you and help you grow. This includes giving to your local church as well as to any individual or organization that is helping you or your family to grow in spiritual ways.

That's a lot of giving, isn't it? But if you are open, God will show you where to direct your giving. The "talents" you've been loaned by the master may be big or small, but you have them. The million-dollar question is "What are you doing with them?" You have the opportunity to take your resources and invest them in the story that God is writing through your life. Like the man who was given five talents, you can do well, and you can expect to hear "Well done" when the master returns to see what you've done with what he's given you. What's stopping you?

WHAT ABOUT YOU?

1. What is the little you have that God might be able to do a lot with?

2. Recall a time when you have been "All in!"

3. Why is it so difficult to give?

4. What great thing would you attempt if you knew you wouldn't fail?

5. What steps can you take to best use your "talents" (your resources) to make a difference in the world?

8

OPPORTUNITY KNOCKS

All of us are heroes in varying degrees. . . .

The hero is defined by his refusal to accept reality . . .

and by a will to alter reality; that is to say, by a will for

adventure. . . . Heroism leads us to resist the impositions of

heredity, of environment. . . . The hero's will is not that of

his ancestors nor of his society, but his own.

—JOSE ORTEGA Y GASSET

In the dark days of December 1941, a troop train was headed for the train station in North Platte, Nebraska. National Guard units were mobilizing for action following the surprise attack on Pearl Harbor, and the community had heard a rumor that the Nebraska National Guard's Company D was scheduled to make a water stop on their way to the West Coast. About five hundred townspeople came to the train station with sandwiches, candy, cigarettes, and letters of encouragement for the boys.

When the train arrived at about five in the afternoon, the crowd hurried toward it. Much to their surprise, it was not Nebraska's Company D but

Company D of the *Kansas* National Guard. After the awkward moment of realization had passed, the gifts were given to the grateful troops, and the train was waved on its way.

A TOWN'S OPPORTUNITY

One woman who was in that crowd was destined to make a difference in the lives of six million soldiers. Her name was Rae Wilson, a twenty-six-year-old drugstore clerk. The following day (December 18) Rae wrote a letter to the now defunct *Daily Bulletin* and encouraged the people of North Platte to make a difference. She wrote,

> I don't know just how many people went to meet the trains when the troops went thru our city on Wednesday, but those who didn't should have. To see the spirits and the high morale among those soldiers should certainly put some of us on our feet and make us realize we are really at war. We should help keep this soldier morale at its highest peak. We can do our part. . . . Why can't we, the people of North Platte and the other towns surrounding our community, start a fund and open a Canteen now? I would be more than willing to give my time without charge and run this canteen. . . . Let's do something and do it in a hurry! We can help this way when we can't help any other way.[1]

Her letter electrified the town and the surrounding communities. From Christmas Day 1941 until the end of World War II four years later, the people of North Platte and the surrounding communities (one hundred twenty-five towns in all) greeted every troop train from five o'clock in the morning until midnight—sometimes up to thirty-two trains per day—with a warm welcome, magazines, baskets of sandwiches, fruit, fried chicken, cakes, and other assorted treats. This effort was amazing on two counts: the era was a time of tight food rationing, *and* the project was staffed entirely by volunteers.

Every day of the year, every day of the war, soldiers ran off the train and were greeted with food and love. Sometimes they enjoyed a quick dance with the local teenagers to the sounds of Glen Miller. Sometimes they enjoyed conversation. But always the soldiers remembered the radical hospitality of the people of North Platte. One survivor of the sunken USS *Lexington* recalled, "You have to understand on that train, you had no bunk. You sat up for three days. You had no shower. You were pretty weary. And then . . . you find this unexpected bouquet of nice people."[2] Often the girls put their names and addresses into popcorn balls or cakes so the boys would have someone to write to. More than a few of these pen pal couples ended up at the marriage altar.

Rae Wilson leveraged her opportunity to make a difference in the lives of six million soldiers. Impact often comes from seeing the same thing everyone else sees (in this case, soldiers with a brief train stop) but thinking something different (*How can we help these soldiers?*) and doing something different. God often presents opportunities that come disguised as problems.

THE CHURCH'S OPPORTUNITY

Many churches today have lost the skill of being part of the fabric of their communities. Whether churches feel like they were run out of town or willingly withdrew, most churches are on the fringes of the communities they seek to impact. Occasionally they make a foray into the city for some search-and-rescue work, but by and large they are isolated from their communities. Christians of earlier centuries were different. The influence and impact of Jesus grew simply because the early Christians saw what everyone else saw—but thought and acted differently.

In a society that devalued children, Christians fashioned themselves after Jesus who welcomed little children. Describing the place of children in early Roman and Greek societies, Baylor professor Rodney Stark writes,

> Far more babies were born than were allowed to live. Seneca regarded the drowning of children at birth as both reasonable and commonplace. . . . It was common to expose an unwanted infant out-of-doors where it could, in principle, be taken up by someone who wished to rear it, but where it typically fell victim to the elements or to animals and birds. Not only was the exposure of infants a very common practice, it was justified by law and advocated by philosophers. Both Plato and Aristotle recommended infanticide as legitimate state policy.[3]

In a city where children were abandoned and left to die, the followers of Christ would comb the city for abandoned babies and raise them and love them as their own. They deplored both abortion and infanticide and swam against the cultural tide by raising their own children and rescuing those children abandoned by others. The number of believers in a given community grew because babies were rescued and raised to be radical followers of Jesus.

Stark notes at least two great plagues in the first three centuries (AD 160 and AD 250) that were instrumental in the church's incredible growth rate, which he estimates at 40 percent per decade. When the plagues came, those who were able fled the city, but the Christians didn't. They stayed and ministered to the sick and dying—Christians and non-Christians alike. Stark observes that just giving basic care of food and water to those too weak to care for themselves would greatly reduce the mortality rate of the victims.

He estimates that 80 percent of Christians survived the plagues compared to only 25 to 50 percent of the general population. So when the plagues subsided, the believers were a substantially higher portion of the population. Beyond this differential in mortality, when non-Christians were nursed to health by believers, and as recipients of such love, they became Christians themselves. When those who fled the city returned to find their loved ones still alive and well, it only increased their admiration of the believers, and many of them became ardent followers of Christ.

People remember how they are treated in the worst of times, when it isn't convenient for someone else to love and serve.

If you are paying attention, God frequently sets opportunities before you. Winds, waves, tremors, and torrents that wreak havoc on lives and property are God's invitation to his people to live out the truths of the story of the Good Samaritan. It's times like these when you enlarge your heart and your arms in reaching out to those who need you.

In times of disaster, *I* and *my* must be replaced with *we* and *our*. And when Christians act like Christ-followers, people are drawn to Jesus. After seeing the organized and cooperative effort of hundreds of churches working together in Louisiana under the banner of PRC Compassion, one official of the Federal Emergency Management Agency (FEMA) said, "This is the best organized relief effort I've ever been a part of. Now I see why it's called 'organized religion.'"[4] If there is ever a time when religion needs to be organized, it is during times when others need help.

INDIVIDUAL OPPORTUNITIES

Before you can change the world, you first must allow the world, with its hurts and need, to change you! Jack Jezreel of JustFaith Ministries defines his work with the old quote: "comforting the afflicted and afflicting the comfortable." Jack works with parishes and dioceses all over the country. He describes his job as "moving people from disinterested to excited involvement."[5]

> *A person who has not been transformed cannot help transform others.*

Jack is full of wisdom and convicting insight. For example, he says that the two "journals" each of us carries are actually spiritual journals. One is a daily planner (or PDA). How we use our time says a lot about our relationship with God. The other is a checkbook ledger. These two journals announce to the world what is really important to us. Ouch! (Well, his job *is* to afflict the comfortable.) Jack points out that the church is a place where people's hearts can be enlarged over and over again. It's a place where you can love people in a bigger way than you could a year ago.

A person who has not been transformed cannot help transform others. Becoming a transformed person does not come from learning more or studying more, but from putting yourself in grace's way, which Jack defines as "putting yourself in positions where God will intersect your life." These intersections happen through across-the-tracks experiences, where we put ourselves in relationships with those on the margins.

Jack speaks of one of his teenage daughters who was spiritually transformed because she spent two months in Haiti one summer simply holding babies who were dying of AIDS. We've all heard powerful sermons and yet not been transformed. We've read great books and yet not been transformed. But how many of us have ministered across the tracks or in a third-world country and have come back the same person?

Across-the-tracks experiences are the best way to grow your heart. Here are some examples.

Lost boys and found men

In the 1980s, the brutal civil war in Sudan led to the massacre of hundreds of thousands of people.[6] Men and older boys were shot while the soldiers took the women and young girls away with them. The young boys who survived (usually between five and eight years of age) banded together and walked hundreds of miles across the open savannah, forged through swollen rivers, foraged for food, and fought off wild animals. Thousands died along the way, but eventually a third of the estimated thirty thousand found their way to refugee camps in Kenya, where they lived on one meal a day for ten years. They were given the name Lost Boys by the refugee workers.

In 2001, three thousand six hundred Lost Boys were welcomed into the United States, and nine of them came to reside in Boulder, Colorado, without lodging, education, or jobs. Jean Wood, a local realtor, saw this as an opportunity to help by finding them housing, enrolling them in school, and getting them jobs. Jean has become "Mom Jean" to the Lost Boys, and she calls them "my guys." For the past few years, Jean has run in the community's BolderBOULDER 10K race with her guys to help raise awareness and finances for the education of these and other Lost Boys (whom she now refers to as Found Men) in the greater Denver area. "I love them all; they are a part of me. I can't imagine my life now without them."

Puppets and prisoners

When Gary Strudler was a Jewish kid growing up in New York, he learned the art of a puppeteer—making inanimate objects come alive.[7] As an elementary school student, he took classes offered by the school district on Saturday mornings and made puppets out of whatever materials he could find. At the age of eight, he began learning the art of ventriloquism. Gary's love for puppetry carried him on through college, where he even took two classes in puppetry on the way to his MA in education from Kent State. His specialty was the large Jim Henson-style puppets that we have seen on *Sesame Street*. After college, via a summer internship, Gary took a job with the Multnomah County Sheriff's Department and moved to Portland. While he was a sheriff there, Gary's life story was intersected by God's story through a neighbor. Gary's neighbor was a Christian who began to talk to him about things that mattered. Gary invited him to be a ride-along during his patrols.

> "I saw a difference in the lives of this guy, his wife, and their friends. I wanted what they had."

Gary says, "I saw a difference in the lives of this guy, his wife, and their friends. I wanted what they had. I tried going back to temple, but that didn't work. My buddy had been asking me if I knew where I would go when I died. And I kept thinking, *Don't all good Jews go to Heaven?* Lying in bed one night at 4:00 AM and pondering Isaiah 53, I told Jesus I would accept him as my Messiah."

Gary eventually was transferred from street patrol to working with schools in a scared-straight type of program sponsored by the Oregon State Penitentiary system. Gary's love for puppetry was rekindled as he began thinking about how he might use his puppets to entertain and minister to those inside the walls, and eventually he was invited to perform his craft inside the prison. So every Christmas and Easter for the past sixteen years, Gary has taken his ad hoc puppet troupe, made up of fifth and sixth graders from his church, into the Oregon State Penitentiary to entertain and tell the story of grace. Typical comments from the prisoners include: "You guys have given me new hope in Jesus," "I'm reading my Bible again," and "I'm walking with the Lord now."

One usually does not think of puppets as agents of grace and transformation, but consider this interesting chain of events: One group of prisoners that Gary ministers to is called the Lifers Club—those who never expect to be released from prison. When the Lifers heard that Gary was organizing a mission trip to Uganda, where he and his young troupe would be ministering, several prisoners crafted seventeen hundred hand puppets to give to the children of Uganda. It was a way they "could give something back." Over the course of this trip, Gary and the fifth and sixth graders performed for over fourteen thousand people and witnessed one thousand of them make commitments to Jesus Christ. Prisoners held captive in their cells had helped bring life to people they would never meet!

The news came that a four-year-old child of the Ugandan missionary who coordinated the trip had cancer. One of the prisoners set up a table in the exercise yard with a sign announcing that he would shave his head if he collected a thousand dollars to be given for the care of this child—not an easy task for prisoners who make thirty cents an hour laboring at prison jobs. Amazingly, the money was raised. But then something even more amazing happened—a prison guard announced that he would shave *his* head if they raised another thousand dollars. The result was two cleanly shaven heads and two thousand dollars! As a puppeteer, Gary brings life into the inanimate. As a Christian, Gary brings life to the lifeless.

Where time stands still

"Imagine walking through a door and finding yourself living more than 1,000 years ago—before electricity, automobiles, and medical services. There are places where you can do just that," says Joe Harvey, spiritual development minister at LifeBridge Christian Church.[8] "There are places where time has passed with very little change over hundreds of years. Places without computers, cable television, and Xboxes. You may ask where these places are, and more importantly, why would anyone want to go there?"

Joe knows of such a place. In February 2003, he took a short-term mission trip there. Joe describes his trip to Loupwalla, a small village in Kenya, as "mind-bending." He writes this of his experience: "Imagine a world in which a mother who gives birth to twins must choose which one to feed and which one to let die. It's happening over there! Imagine a place where superstitions drive people to live in fear of offending dead ancestors. Consider what it would be like to lie down outside on a woven mat each night in a place known for its spitting cobras and 3-inch scorpions. . . . It's a real place where the average life expectancy is 47 years."

This short-term mission trip brought perspective to the travelers as well as help to the missionaries and the villagers.

Does this sound dreadful? Oddly enough, people live in this place and enjoy friendships and family ties. They find ways to laugh, play, and dream for better days to come. Those better days are coming in no small part because of people like Kip and Katy Lines, missionaries who invest in the future of these distant people. Joe shares, "I used to think of missionaries as long-distance preachers and teachers. They are that, but they are so much more. They provide community benevolence, emergency medical support and transportation, literacy training, and help develop plans for social and economic improvement. Most importantly, they bring the comfort and hope that can only come from God."

"Talking with the Lineses," Joe says, "I learned about their joys and sorrows. It's hard to live thousands of miles from family and friends, and the feeling of isolation can sometimes be overwhelming. Then there are the difficulties of relating to a different culture and dealing with unrealistic expectations. The many downsides also include coping with health risks like the ever-present malaria. The odds of remaining healthy in such a place seem impossible, but Kip and Katy have been spared from serious illnesses. Beyond the challenges, they saw an opportunity to serve God's purposes with compassion and faithfulness. They became an integral part of the lives of these people and have seen lives changed and faith develop. I came to admire their dependent courage and their vision for how God could use their lives to extend his love and grace to others."

If you ask Joe about his trip, he will most certainly tell you about his realization of the importance of taking God's message of love and hope, but he will also tell you how it added a new dimension to his own faith. This short-term mission trip brought perspective to the travelers as well as help to the missionaries and the villagers. "Like all growth opportunities, there is a correlation between risk and reward. It's hard to put yourself in the center of a foreign culture. On the other hand, it's only there that you find the perspective to evaluate your own. It is only then that some aspects of your faith become challenged or crystal clear."

Giving people fish . . . and fishing lessons

Kathy Greer of Creekside Community Church in San Leandro, California, describes her position as a happy volunteer.[9] She is Creekside's volunteer coordinator for an elementary school in Oakland, located a mile and a half from the church. Kathy operates under a "fish" philosophy: giving a person a fish is sustenance for a day, and teaching people to fish provides sustenance for a lifetime.

Kathy knows how to bless people by giving them fish. For the past three years, Creekside has hosted seven teacher-appreciation events for the seventy-five teachers and the staff of the school. Each teacher and staff member receives a beautiful invitation to the event, and when they arrive they receive a gift bag filled with things they can use and enjoy. Kathy says, "After our first event an elderly teacher came up and said, 'I've been in this school thirty-two years, and apart from the time we got a mimeographed memo in our box, this is the only appreciation we've ever received.' Teachers stop me in the hall and tell me, 'If no one has told you, I want to tell you how much we appreciate Creekside. Everything you do means so much to us.'" Kids stop Kathy and other volunteers in the hall and say, "Hey, you're with that church that gave us the backpacks."

Kathy knows how to bless people with fish. But most of her satisfaction comes from the way the people of Creekside have been able to teach other people *how* to fish. In April 2004 a teacher stopped Kathy and told her, "I just want to tell you that we just finished a week of teacher-parent conferences and every parent that has a child in your tutoring program was glowing and couldn't say enough about how a person at Creekside had impacted their child this year." Teaching kids to read is empowerment for life.

Kathy acknowledges that although the Creekside helpers can't directly share Christ with the students, they are making a kingdom difference.

A business executive from Creekside found that he had a heart for the poor of his community. Like other high-capacity leaders, he didn't ask himself how he could ladle soup more efficiently, but rather, *Why are there so many people in the soup line?* His part of the solution was to start a ministry called Career Hope, through which he teaches the community's unemployed and underemployed things like computer skills, interviewing, and résumé writing, along with life skills essential to bettering oneself. He is teaching them to fish.

Warden Green

When you think of a jail warden, a tough and sometimes corrupt individual (as portrayed in movies like *The Shawshank Redemption* and *Brubaker*) comes to mind. It's easy to see how someone in this line of work would become cynical and distrusting, but not Rob Green. He defies the Hollywood picture of a warden every day. This forty-one-year-old husband and father is the warden of the Montgomery County Jail in Maryland. He's not particularly warm and fuzzy, but Rob knows how to "see" people.

He chooses to see the eight hundred inmates in his jail on any given day as the fathers, sons, mothers, and daughters that they are. For the past six years, he has made it a priority that the inmates learn life skills through productive programs. Over 70 percent of his jail population participate in opportunities for education, literacy, substance abuse treatment, résumé and work skills training. Rob says, "I see myself as a good soldier, but I never want to dehumanize anyone." It's been a rule of his since beginning his career in corrections over twenty years ago.

While Warden Green leads the charge, he acknowledges that none of this would be possible without others also choosing to value the incarcerated men and women of Montgomery County. "We have seventy-five churches currently engaging volunteers in our jail programs." Rob believes that these volunteers are what make all the difference because he has the stats to prove it. Most jails see at least one thousand altercations in two months' time. "We had thirty-one altercations in our jail in the past sixty days. Our biggest conflict was between two inmates fighting over what to watch on educational television—a program about the history of the pyramids or *Animal Planet*," says Rob. "Volunteers serving in the jail bring a sense of acceptance and a reminder that society has not forgotten about them." This is a critical step toward successful reentry into the community. To Rob, the ministry that happens in jail is vital, "but just showing up and saying 'here's a Bible' just isn't enough." Rob believes in living out faith.

Not all of the volunteers working with the jail actually visit the jail. "There are kind women who make themselves available to visit an inmate's mother in the nursing home and report her status back to her son in the jail." Many times, when a father is incarcerated, there is a family sitting in the waiting room with no place to go. "We have volunteers who come and help these mothers find temporary housing or food during this confusing and difficult time," he says.

But it's not all milk and cookies in the Montgomery County Jail. There are boundaries, and the inmates in Rob's jail know that. "It is a privilege to be in our programs. If someone messes up and disrespects a volunteer or instructor or doesn't show up to the program, there is a thirty-day waiting period before he or she can reenter a program. I never waive it."

Rob's personal life echoes the same passion for people as his professional life does. On any given Friday night, you'll find Rob and his young son sitting down with men at the local men's mission, eating a monster sub sandwich he brought to share. For just a moment, the men at the mission feel normal as they share a sandwich, watch Rob's son play, and talk sports. "I want to show my son what it means to care and give back."

Growing up with an alcoholic father and an unavailable mother, Rob knows firsthand what it's like to come from a difficult home life. "Every day I go to work, I am humbled," Rob states. He realizes that each of us is just a situation away from making a desperate choice—like many of the inmates he sees day in and day out. He's thankful for the grandparents who raised him and taught him the value of hard work on the farm.

Rob views his work as extending beyond the bars. When he found out that the local school district paid forty-seven thousand dollars a year to have their school buses cleaned and serviced, he saw the opportunity he'd been looking for with his weekend inmates—the men who work and live in regular society but are sentenced to serve time each weekend for their crimes. Instead of having these men just sit for forty-eight hours, Rob knew that they could be a value to the community and learn to take pride in meaningful work. He arranged for the weekend inmates to clean and service the buses. Because of this intersection between the jail and the school district, the district was able to hire another teacher with the forty-seven thousand dollars saved.

Finding innovative solutions to problems is a daily occurrence for Rob. He allows his story to intersect with others every day in the Montgomery County Jail and beyond. With his jail fully programmed, he is now engaging in a better, more effective reentry program for inmates leaving jail. He helps former inmates get governmental IDs that double as a bus pass so they can make it to their parole meetings and get a job. "This," says Rob, "is the most important work I've ever done in my career." He is changing the stories of prisoners, one inmate at a time.

Rockin' Bosnia

On any given weekend night in Banja Luka, Bosnia, you might find Sheila Berg singing with her all-girl rock band ORT.[10] If you look past the crowd and through the blanket of smoke that hovers underneath the café's low ceiling, you'll probably find her husband, Scoggins, standing around a high-top table with some friends.

As Sheila says, "We're not Bosnian. But all of our friends here are. We came to this Eastern European town three and a half years ago as missionaries, sent out by our church [Lifespring Christian] in Cincinnati, Ohio. No one expected that I'd end up on stage, singing in the local language and making friendships to last a lifetime. No one, I suppose, but God."[11] During the day Sheila helps Scoggins run a small humanitarian aid organization in the town. One evening a week Sheila practices with fellow band mates Danijela, Nevena, and Milica. Sheila explains, "Being a part of their world, a professional musician in the local music scene, has given me the chance to be myself and let God grow our relationships naturally." This natural intersection of their lives led to Sheila's starting a Bible study with the girls.

ORT just placed fourth in an international songwriting competition and was awarded the title Best New Band. But Sheila says the awards and accolades are not the best part of her experience with the band. It's "being involved in people's lives on their turf and in their comfort zone." She continues, "I never asked the girls to come and join a band that I was creating, a band that would sing only Christian songs and that would play in church basements. I love being in the trenches with my friends, and I wouldn't have it any other way. I love sharing life with them, sharing about God, and sharing the hope that he brings."

> *"No one expected that I'd end up on stage, singing in the local language and making friendships to last a lifetime. No one, I suppose, but God."*

That's what it's all about—creating intersections God can use to draw people to himself, then seizing opportunities and using them to influence others' stories.

Opportunities for entrepreneurs

Peter Drucker tells us that the term *entrepreneur* was defined over two hundred years ago by a French economist as someone who "shifts economic resources out of an area of lower and into an area of higher productivity and greater yield."[11] Entrepreneurs see the world differently than most people. Where most people see problems, entrepreneurs see opportunities. Where most people think incremental growth, entrepreneurs think exponential growth. Entrepreneurs are not bound to an effort-equals-results way of thinking. They think in terms of leverage—how to get the best results in the shortest amount of time, the greatest results for the least effort. Entrepreneurs organize the world differently. They simply see things about the future that others only recognize after they are a reality.

Entrepreneurs are those rare individuals who create new value by weaving together underutilized assets or opportunities into something that never existed before. In God's kingdom, entrepreneurs take the five talents given to them by the master and multiply them to ten, only to be given more again. They are the church planters who don't ask "How can we raise the money to start thirty churches?" but rather "How can we start thirty churches without any money?" Entrepreneurs have a way of changing the equation and, in the process, changing our world. Entrepreneurs look for singular solutions that solve multiple problems.

Social entrepreneurs are even more innovative, for they seek not just one bottom line but two bottom lines—making money *and* making a difference.

One such entrepreneur is Jim Reiner, executive director of Belay Enterprises in Denver, Colorado. Since 1995, Belay's mission has been "to partner with area churches to develop businesses that employ and job-train individuals rebuilding lives from addiction, homelessness, prison, and poverty in order to strengthen families and neighborhoods."[12]

Belay's board consists of people from the business sector as well as local pastors. Under Jim's leadership, Belay has developed and spawned a number of growing businesses as ministries that are not only changing lives but also making money. Take Bud's Warehouse, for example. The founders of Bud's (builders and pastors) recognized that Colorado's construction boom was generating hundreds of over-ordered items, from doors to sinks to cabinets to bathtubs—most of which were taken to a landfill following the end of a construction project. That's what they noticed as entrepreneurs. As compassionate believers, they had noticed something else; they had come face-to-face with the hopeless and the people of Denver most difficult to employ—the homeless, ex-offenders, the uneducated, alcoholics, and addicts.

Putting these two disparate issues together was the beginning of Bud's Warehouse, a building materials warehouse that sells quality building products from 30 to 70 percent below retail cost. Last year Bud's Warehouse generated over one million dollars in sales. But more than that, Bud's is turning lives around, employing up to eighteen of the hardest-to-employ people (a good résumé is a disqualifier for being hired by Bud's). Bud's pays from eight to ten dollars per hour, with an impressive 52 percent of the employees graduating to better-paying jobs in the community. Employees come from referrals by local urban churches or human service agencies.

> *Last year Bud's Warehouse generated over one million dollars in sales. But more than that, Bud's is turning lives around.*

Every day begins at eight thirty in the morning with Bible reading and a short time of prayer. Though employees are not required to attend, most of them find themselves wanting to be part of a larger community. The work program has three phases: Phase 1 focuses on the soft skills of employment—showing up on time, customer service, and goal setting. Phase 2 focuses on learning the business through skill development and training. Phase 3 focuses on readying employees for employment in the marketplace through résumé preparation and interview skills.

Another entrepreneurial business that Jim started is Baby Bud's—a job-training program for disadvantaged single mothers. Baby Bud's specializes in gently used maternity clothing and baby and toddler clothing at a savings of up to 70 percent. Women employed at Baby Bud's also participate in a six- to twelve-month three-phase program during which they are equipped to graduate to better jobs in the community with improved life and career skills. Baby Bud's was recently named Best Place to Buy Baby Stuff of Aurora, Colorado.

Recognizing that having a car is absolutely essential to entering the growing suburban job market, Belay Enterprises launched Good Neighbor Garage in 2003. Mechanics in a job-training program repair cars that are then sold for a modest client fee to their program graduates, single moms, and families who can improve their lives through better employment opportunities. In 2005 Good Neighbor Garage expected to provide seventy-five cars to better the lives of the people in Denver. If necessity is the mother of invention, then apparently entrepreneurs are the fathers.

Perhaps the most innovative feature of Belay Enterprises is the Ascent Venture Fund—a venture account funded by donations and profits spun off from Bud's Warehouse. Jim fully expects to launch one hundred neighborhood businesses in the next five years through his microlending project.

Our world needs entrepreneurs. But more importantly, we need social and spiritual entrepreneurs who put together new value equations for the kingdom. We need people who see the choice not in terms of business *or* ministry but business *as* ministry.

OPPORTUNITIES ABOUND

Bud's Warehouse and Belay Enterprises are pretty unique combinations of business and ministry. Do you think such big projects are out of reach for you? Remember the principle from the previous chapter— small things you do can make a huge difference. How can you begin to think like a ministry entrepreneur? How can you leverage your opportunities—big ones and small ones—for God?

When God created the heavens and the earth, he made everything using only three geometrical shapes—circles, rectangles, and triangles. He used three colors. Every color in the hues under Heaven is made up of some combination of the three primary colors—red, yellow, and blue. God also made everything out of three types of matter—solid, liquid, and gas. Look around you! Everything you see, no matter how complex, consists in some configuration of these shapes, colors, or forms of matter. If God can do so much with so little, imagine what he can do through you!

When God placed Adam and Eve in the Garden of Eden, he gave them opportunities and potential—animals to name and plants that would produce seeds for reproduction. Everything they needed was there before them. They were in partnership with God, totally equipped to accomplish his will. It's hard to imagine that even though God has placed us here with so many opportunities and so much potential, we would opt to keep sitting on the sidelines.

Get in the game, join God in what he is doing—and grow to be like him in the process! Opportunity awaits.

WHAT ABOUT YOU?

1. Where have you seen one person make all the difference in the lives of many others?

2. What opportunities, which currently may be seen as problems, are in front of you today?

3. How can God use these adverse situations to further his plan in the lives of others?

4. Where do you see underutilized assets, or connections to be made, that could have great potential for the kingdom?

5. What will you do about it?

ETERNITY

A friend of ours keeps an enormous jar of marbles on his desk at work. Each marble represents a Saturday of his life that his kids are still living at home. Saturdays, then, are for playing catch, visiting the zoo, swimming at the local pool, picnicking in the park, taking in a baseball game, driving to the mountains, and being a fan and cheerleader of whatever his kids love to do. Each Monday morning he removes a marble from the jar, and with each passing year he has fifty-two fewer marbles in the jar.

There is a day coming, right before the graduation of his youngest daughter, when there will be only one marble left in the jar. When he pulls that last marble out, though the jar will be empty, his life will be full of memories, laughter, and joy because he made every marble count. Moses said, "The length of our days is seventy years— or eighty, if we have the strength; . . . for they quickly pass, and we fly away" (Psalm 90:10).

Time is but a small slice of eternity on loan from God—but it can have significance that lasts forever. William Blake wrote, "Eternity is in love with the productions of time."[1] Each of us has enough time to accomplish what God wants us to accomplish and to love everyone he wants us to love. One day we'll reach into our jars and there will be no more marbles; we will step over the threshold into eternity.

9
TIME, A SLICE OF ETERNITY

*Time is too slow for those who wait, too swift for those who
fear, too long for those who grieve, too short for those who
rejoice, but for those who love, time is eternity.*

—HENRY VAN DYKE

L ife is full of tiny moments that—we realize upon reflection—
become very big moments. We never know how a particular
moment or event will shape the future and have a huge impact.

Consider the story of Alfred Nobel. A pacifist by tempera-
ment but an inventor by nature, in 1866 at the age of thirty-three, he
patented the process of turning nitroglycerin into dynamite. He thought
the invention would end all wars, that knowledge of its explosive power
would cause people to cringe at the very idea of war. He was wrong. Soon
dynamite's deadly force was used to annihilate thousands. In 1888, when
Alfred's brother Ludvig died, the local newspaper mistakenly published
Alfred's obituary, in which he was referred to as "the merchant of death."

Few people have the opportunity to see firsthand how they will be
remembered—but Alfred did. Not wanting to be remembered as the

merchant of death, he redirected the course and cause of his life. When he died in 1896, friends and relatives were shocked to read his sealed will. Alfred left approximately 94 percent of his worth to the establishment of five prizes for "those who, during the preceding year, shall have conferred the greatest benefit on mankind."[1] These prizes have become known as the Nobel Prizes and have been awarded every year since 1901 to the leaders in the fields of physics, chemistry, physiology or medicine, literature, and peace.

> *It might not be that your moments seem particularly spectacular to you, but in God's eternal perspective, every moment in time counts and is a special gift on loan.*

Alfred's name is now and forever associated with peace, not death. Reading his own epitaph involved only a small moment of Alfred's time, but it has had great consequences.

It might not be that your moments seem particularly spectacular to you, but in God's eternal perspective, every moment in time counts and is a special gift on loan.

Hurricane Katrina brought America's worst national disaster in nearly one hundred years. As the storm winds blew and floodwaters rose, people in the city of New Orleans and other places in the Gulf Coast area began to realize how tragic this storm would be. The resulting flood shut down the city of New Orleans for weeks.

Stories continue to pour forth from this disaster, stories that are a mixture of triumph and tragedy, heroism and terrorism. It is in a disaster like this that we see demonstrated both the best and the worst of mankind. The early hours gave rise to heroics, like people sacrificing their own lives to save their friends or family members, and strangers doing house-to-house searches for the stranded or medically fragile. It was also those early hours that gave rise to the rampant looting and preying on those who were unable to defend themselves. We are capable of using our moments for good or for ill, to help or to harm, to be selfless or selfish.

I (Rick) have the privilege of serving on a board that helps provide care for individuals who have mental retardation and developmental disabilities. We have twenty-two homes in and around the New Orleans area. The individuals in those homes faced unbelievable disruption in their lives. Without the tireless sacrifice of many, these people would have been unable to flee the storm before it arrived, but all of them were evacuated well ahead of the storm.

Thousands of others in the city of New Orleans either were unable or unwilling to evacuate the city. As a result, the Superdome in New Orleans (which has played host to many world-famous sporting events) became home to thousands of refugees. More than fifteen thousand people sought refuge in this massive makeshift shelter. The needs of those refugees were overwhelming.

Fox National News reported that after several days in this arena without electricity or running water, the most requested item from those stranded in the Superdome was a Bible. Most of the people had lost all they had; many had lost family and friends. They were residing in a temporary shelter that was, at best, less than adequate. They were eating military ready-to-eat meals and drinking bottled water. They could have asked to be supplied with any number of things, yet the most requested item was the Bible.

SEE BEYOND THE MOMENT

Does that seem odd to you? With all of the urgent and pressing needs in the face of great loss and tragedy, they wanted a book. But not just any book—they wanted the book that would reveal God, the book that tells God's story, the book that invites us to see beyond this moment and into eternity (which is just a moment away). They wanted the book that gives hope to the hopeless, brings light to the darkness, and calm to the chaos. They asked for the book that invites us to see beyond circumstances and reminds us that our stories matters.

It is often in crisis that we are forced (or maybe just given the opportunity) to see the bigger picture of life. It is in moments of chaos, not calm, that we often realize God's gift of time to us. In moments of disaster, the things that matter seem to come into focus fairly quickly. Somewhere within us, we recognize that there is something bigger than we are. It is in the middle of the storm that we look for an anchor; it's when life seems fragile that we look for stability. And often when our moments seem so temporary, we look for the eternal.

The Bible invites you to see beyond this moment. The apostle Paul observed, "We fix our eyes not on what is seen, but on what is unseen. For what is seen is temporary, but what is unseen is eternal" (2 Corinthians 4:18). Paul is talking about focus. The phrase "fix our eyes" comes from the word *skopos*, the same root in our words *telescope* and *microscope*. It means "to look at one thing to the exclusion of other things." "Fix your eyes" pertains to what really captures your attention. What is your primary focus in life? What are you building your life around— what is seen or what is unseen? the temporary or the eternal?

It doesn't have to be a hurricane or flooded city that causes you to look beyond the moment. The personal hurricanes you face can be enough to make you ask yourself, *Is this what I want? How will I go forward from this place?* A job loss, health issue, divorce, death, or just a change in your circumstances can create enough momentum for you to wonder, *What am I doing?*

The apostle Paul wrote, "[God's] intent was that now, through the church [*which is you and me*], the manifold wisdom of God should be made known . . . according to his eternal purpose which he accomplished in Christ Jesus our Lord" (Ephesians 3:10, 11). How can your life have an eternal impact? How can you make the most of your slice of time?

My friend Dr. Leroy Lawson says the best way to know if you are doing God's will is to ask two questions: "What has God given you to give away?" and "Who needs it?" Those two questions are a great way to zero in on the journey of living a life on loan. What do you have, and who can use it? This goes way beyond the possessions that you could give to someone. It's more than giving *things*, even though in previous chapters we learned that being less attached to possessions is a good thing.

When you view your life as not your own, you see your moments, your experiences, your abilities, your successes, your failures . . . everything as part of your story.

When you view your life as not your own, you see your moments, your experiences, your abilities, your successes, your failures . . . everything as part of your story. God even sees you, yourself, as a gift that can be given—in his name and for his eternal purpose—to benefit others.

What has God provided that you can pass on to others? We've already discussed how God has given each of us material possessions, unique experiences, and opportunities for influence—all of which we can use for him. Doing anything for God also requires our time, which is another thing God has given us. Let's look at some practical steps you can use to assess each of these items in your life. In living a life on loan, you personally invite God to help you make some choices about these significant gifts he has given you to give away.

POSSESSIONS

We've already talked a lot about how your money and your things can be given to benefit others. One thing to remember is that you should experience joy in giving away your treasure. People who are generous with God's resources experience the joy of giving. Jesus said, "It is more blessed to give than to receive" (Acts 20:35). The giver always receives more than he or she gives. Jesus also said, "Give, and it will be given to you. A good measure, pressed down, shaken together and running over, will be poured into your lap. For with the measure you use, it will be measured to you" (Luke 6:38).

A rich young ruler approached Jesus and asked how he could have eternal life. After Jesus gave his answer, the Bible says, "Jesus looked at him and loved him. 'One thing you lack,' he said. 'Go, sell everything you have and give to the poor, and you will have treasure in heaven. Then come, follow me'" (Mark 10:21).

Jesus didn't want to wreck the man's life. He wanted to make it better! Everything Jesus asked him to do was motivated by a deep sense of love for this man.

How did this wealthy man respond? "At this the man's face fell. He went away sad, because he had great wealth" (v. 22). The man went away sad, when he could have gone away filled with joy. Albert Schweitzer, the doctor and missionary to Africa, said, "If there is something that you own that you cannot give away, you don't own it. It owns you."[2]

I (Rick) had traveled to New York City for a meeting. My wife Diane went along with me, and we met up with some good friends during our visit. One of them wanted to see a Broadway show, so we tried to get tickets. But as often happens in New York, a couple of shows we wanted to see were sold out. We ended up going to see *Moving On*, featuring the music of Billy Joel; however, we unknowingly purchased obstructed-view-seat tickets. What should have been explained to us was that these seats were for people from out of town who don't have any other option, are suckers, and will pay too much for tickets!

During the very first number, the band was lifted on a riser and went up . . . somewhere. From where we were seated, who knows where they went! They could have been playing a CD for all we knew. About ten minutes into the show, I leaned over to Diane and said, "You know, I don't really have any interest in this. I think I'll go." Trust me, that wasn't a good thing to say. "I can go back to the hotel room, plug a CD in, and get the same experience we're getting here." But I didn't get the response I wanted, so I stayed for the show. So there we were in the back row of the second balcony. I know you're going to be surprised by this, but I was pouting a little about the whole thing.

Finally, the show was over and the band came back down (proof they *had* been in the building the whole time). Suddenly, cameras started coming out, and people were getting all excited. Billy Joel himself had walked in to celebrate the second anniversary of the show's opening. No one knew he was coming—at least no one on stage seemed to know, and certainly nobody in the audience knew.

Even with our obstructed-view seats, we got to watch him do a fifteen-minute impromptu performance. It was very cool and the highlight of the evening. But I would have missed it if I had gotten my way earlier in the show when I couldn't see.

The rich young ruler thought he'd seen and heard enough. But he should have stayed with Jesus. Even though he didn't have spiritual eyes to see clearly, he could have learned more about handling his treasure, how to be generous, and how to live with less money but more perspective. Instead, his attitude about possessions stood in the way—and he left too soon.

EXPERIENCES

Where you have been, what you have learned, and what you have experienced deeply matter. This is probably one of the hardest aspects of living a life on loan. It's hard to imagine that God can (and will) use even the bad experiences, the trash in your life—whether the trash was dumped on you or you created it yourself. Yes, even your pain has come into your life so that you can give something away. Your heartaches and accomplishments, your joys and sorrows can provide just what someone else needs.

Be honest. It is the disappointments and heartaches that cause you to grow the most. Can you point to your own pain and see how it can assist others in their journeys and help change their life stories?

You heard the first part of my (Rick's) mom's story in chapter 1 of this book. She really had it rough growing up—with abandonment, alcohol, and other issues. But her disappointments didn't end with her childhood. My mom, Sharon, lost three children to the Rh-negative blood disorder, and then she lost a fourth child when my sister Darcy, at age eighteen, was killed in an automobile accident by a drunk driver.

This sorrow upon sorrow would cause many to give up, cave in, or find a way to avoid the pain. My mom chose, however, to live through the pain and to look for healing. She took her grief and found an outlet for it in helping others. She became a grief counselor with a group called Hope for Bereaved.[3] In this way she not only provided practical help but also could point to her path as an encouragement to others.

My mom can honestly say, "I cannot know what you are feeling because none of us can know exactly another person's emotions. I recognize the road you're on, because I have been on that road. There is light, there is hope, and there is healing."

When heartache and disappointment come, you can, as so many have suggested, get better or get bitter. Those who choose to get better can be a gift to others who are struggling or hurting. We all have hurts. You can pick at your wound, allowing it to fester and grow with infection, or you can choose to let it heal. You can stay focused on the hurts (the who, how, and what happened), or you can choose to focus on getting healed and helping others in the time you have.

I have a scar on the palm of my hand. Every time I notice it, I am instantly reminded of how it got there. I was about twelve years old when I was running through the woods behind my house. I tripped on a log and, in an attempt to break my fall, put my hands out only to have my right hand land on a broken soda bottle. The glass cut deep and right through a small vein, which wouldn't stop bleeding. One emergency room and five stitches later, I was on my way home. I hurt. The cut hurt, the stitches hurt, the antiseptic hurt . . . and I cried. It took a little while for the wound to heal, but eventually it did. Now I have a scar. No pain, no blood, no wound—just a scar.

If you could see into my heart, you would see a number of emotional scars. They are in all kinds of shapes and sizes. When I notice them, I am reminded of how they got there. Some of the details are vivid, and a lot are faded or just distant memories. These scars have been accumulated over the years—some I've caused, some others have caused, and some are just the way life goes. They aren't what I would have chosen, and many aren't fair or just, but they are there just the same.

When these wounds were fresh, a few seemed unbearable; some were just nicks. Even after a complete healing, a scar may remain. And all scars have a story. We can live with our scars. And we can use them. There is something very peculiar that happens when we use our painful experiences to serve others. Healing often comes through serving.

Christmas can be the most wonderful time of the year (as the song goes). But for some, it can be the absolute worst time of the year. Painful reminders of broken marriages, memories of lost loved ones, or simple loneliness surface in that long season from Thanksgiving through New Year's Day. It was near Christmastime when my sister died; since her death, Christmas has always been bittersweet for my family. When there is the potential for so much pain, how can serving others during the holiday season bring about healing?

There is healing power and hope when you give of yourself. That power really can't be explained, except to acknowledge that it is part of God's eternal purpose.

Christmas is supposed to be a magical time with decorations, celebrations, and lots of light. There wasn't much light for Tammy the year she got divorced. Her ex-husband had the kids, and she was totally alone on Christmas Eve for the very first time in her life. Add to that the fact that she was in the worst financial shape she had ever been in. The holidays weren't turning out to be very merry or bright. What did she do? She decided to serve.

She volunteered through a local nonprofit organization to deliver Christmas gifts to families in need. Instead of sitting home alone in the dark, she decided to be a light to others. Through being a light that Christmas, she was grateful despite her depressing situation.

No matter what your circumstances, God can use you to be a light to others. "The people walking in darkness have seen a great light; on those living in the land of the shadow of death a light has dawned" (Isaiah 9:2). What was this great light the people saw? It was Jesus Christ. Seven hundred years before Christ's birth, Isaiah foretold his coming. When there is no other light in your life, he promises to be one. Often the light gets brighter when you give yourself away as he did.

Steve teaches at a residential treatment facility for troubled teens. As part of their treatment and rehabilitation, these teens are encouraged to participate in community service. This isn't community service they've necessarily been sentenced to, but for these teens, everything in life seems like a sentence. They come to the facility very broken in spirit, often addicted to a substance, or rebellious beyond their parents' control.

Steve and a small group of boys were on a service project for a local inner-city church in Denver. They were painting and doing some minor repairs to the property. When lunchtime came, the small band of servants was fed a meal and had the opportunity to meet some of the older people in the church. With all sincerity one lady said to the boys, "You are an answer to prayer! Thank you so much for coming today." On their ride home, Steve commented to the boys, "I bet none of you ever thought you would be an answer to somebody's prayer!" And it's so true! This group of juvenile delinquents had probably never been labeled as anything other than "trouble." Serving others gave them a new label—"an answer to prayer"—and helped initiate the healing and recovery process.

There is healing power and hope when you give of yourself. That power really can't be explained, except to acknowledge that it is part of God's eternal purpose and that there are always multitudes of blessing when you serve others and live your life—on loan *from* God—*for* God.

What about the wounds on your heart? Are they keeping you from living a life on loan for God? Your scars—if you allow them to heal—have a story. You will always have the scars, but you can live with the scars. Rick Warren says, "God never wastes a hurt!"[4] The things you have done or things that have been done to you might very well be painful (maybe even horrible), but they don't have to be wasted. Those experiences can be used to help others. What you have learned, how you have journeyed, or just the fact that somehow you have survived can be the very thing that someone else might need.

INFLUENCE

You can use your influence for the benefit of others. A young woman once used her influence to save an entire nation from genocide. God placed the young girl Esther into a situation where she became a queen. Seeing her God-given opportunity to make a difference, Esther took it. The king spared the lives of the Jewish men, women, and children in his kingdom just as the order to annihilate them was being written. It took a great amount of Esther's courage to approach the king and to use her influence, but her cousin Mordecai reminded her, "Who knows but that you have come to royal position for such a time as this?" (Esther 4:14).

Even though Esther had no royal heritage, God made a path for her to serve his purposes by influencing the court of the king. What path of influence could God be setting before you?

Someday your somedays will be over. There will be a day when you draw your last breath. More than likely, people will gather together in a church or chapel or some other meaningful place, and there will be a funeral service for you. At the service a minister will get up and say nice things about you (even if he has to do some creative writing). After the service those people will gather together in a fellowship hall or someone's living room and eat potato salad. While they are eating, they will talk about you—really talk about your influence on their lives.

What will be said about what you have done? When people remember you, what will they say about how you spent your moments? How will you have used your slice of eternity to connect people to God's grace?

Daddy Bruce's barbecued ribs, chicken, and brisket were something to wait in line for at his ramshackle restaurant in Denver.[5] The sauce was tangy and not too sweet—perfect for the three-meat combo. Daddy Bruce served it to you on a compartmentalized foam plate with a side of potato salad and two slices of white bread. And if you wanted it to go, he'd put a piece of foil over the plate and hand it to you with a smile. If you had several plates of food, he'd provide a cardboard box for carrying them out.

The restaurant was never a five-star establishment, but the owner, Bruce Randolph, was a five-star man. When he passed away at the age of ninety-four, the Denver Broncos paid the funeral costs, for he was quite a fan. He was carried to his resting place in a donated Cadillac and buried in a donated suit, for he died penniless. More than a thousand people came to pay their final respects to a man originally from Arkansas who called himself "only a cooker." Daddy Bruce was legendary in the Denver area for his generosity. It was said that if you showed up for lunch and were short on money . . . well, that was OK because Daddy Bruce didn't feel that it was right for anyone to be hungry.

Every Thanksgiving for over thirty years, the poor, the hungry, and the homeless had arrived at his restaurant and lined up en masse for their best meal of the year, cooked by Daddy Bruce and served by volunteers from all over the city.

Those who had once stood in line and those who had served in line now lined up to pay their last respects to Denver's penniless philanthropist. The mayor called him a legend. The state of Colorado sent a letter signed by the governor. Denver's chief of police and other city officials crowded in to say their final thanks and farewell to a man who left the world a little bit better off than he found it.

In the end, the man with only a third-grade education was granted an honorary doctorate of humane letters from the University of Colorado and had a middle school in Denver named in his honor. The man who gave so much away and died with nothing had a street named after him—Bruce Randolph Avenue. One man who had little more than a big heart gave so much. His influence was immeasurable. "The memory of the righteous will be a blessing" (Proverbs 10:7).

TIME

Both of us live near Boulder, Colorado, home to the International Standard Atomic Clock. It so accurately measures time that the world sets its timepieces by this mechanism. Today you can buy a watch that at four o'clock every morning will recalibrate itself to the atomic clock in Boulder no matter where you are in the world. The atomic clock is so accurate that it measures fractions of seconds called femtoseconds.

Although we're all given a mere twenty-four hours in a day, we always have enough time to do exactly what God wants us to do!

The clock keeps track of time with such precision that every few years a leap second needs to be added to our day to maintain its accuracy. Since 1972, seventeen such leap seconds have been added to the clock to maintain its timely integrity.[6]

Wow! Seventeen seconds have been given to me as a gift. What did I do with this gift of time? OK, seventeen seconds doesn't seem like enough to do anything with. Still, most of us wish we could be given more time.

- More time with my spouse
- More one-on-one time with a friend
- More time to attend my kids' activities and competitions
- More quality time *with* my kids
- More time away from my busy schedule
- More time to determine where my passion and purpose intersect

The one thing we seem to need more of is time, but time is one of those fixed entities (like matter) that can neither be created (with the notable exception of the leap second) nor destroyed; nor can it be stored up for future use. If ever there were an object to which "use it or lose it" applies, that object is time. Although we're all given a mere twenty-four hours in a day, we always have enough time to do exactly what God wants us to do!

Is it time for a priority check of how you use your time? Rare is the person who wouldn't describe himself or herself as busy. As a society, we rush from one thing to another while doing something in between. When you ask someone "How are you doing today?" a common response is "I'm busy." Being busy is somehow equated with worth. If you are busy, then you must be needed, useful, important. Multitasking is a badge of honor for most of us.

What do you do when you are busy? If you are like many, you start making a list of all the things you are doing; then you decide you are going to get your life and schedule in order. So you go over your list, cross out what you're not going to do, and quit doing those things.

- Coach little league
- PTA
- Exercise three times a week
- ~~Bake cookies for band camp~~
- Paint the guest room
- ~~Have a garage sale~~

If you are really good and have attended time management seminars, you'll even begin to prioritize the list. (I used to teach time management seminars. I know how this works.)

- Clean house—B
- Walk the dog—A
- Do homework—A
- Bring photo albums up to date—C

If you are really, really good, then you'll number your priorities— A1, A2, B1, B3 . . .

How long does that work? A week? A month? Not long enough—that is for sure! It is kind of like cleaning out the garage—after a while it's full of stuff and cobwebs again.

If you're like most people, you either have a hard time keeping your priorities or tend to add new activities to the list until you are really busy again. But I would suggest that your problem isn't your list or your ability to get things done; it is that you start at the wrong end of the stick.

Try this simple formula that can help you make sense out of the busyness. This isn't new, or original with me, and is a part of many personal management strategies in one form or another. It is useful and can be a powerful exercise for you to do, especially if you're too busy. It starts with a simple formula: P–G–A (and, no, it has very little to do with the Professional Golfers Association).

P–G–A

P is for purposes

To-be statements are good purpose statements. These assertions give direction to your life and will help you formulate what's most important to you. Here are some general to-be statements: "I want to be a better spouse," "I want to be a more effective leader," "I want to be an accomplished musician."

Purpose statements give a general sense of the direction you are heading, as if you were saying, for example, "I'm going west, not north!" They aren't specific enough to actually complete a task, and they certainly don't give you an action plan for accomplishment. But they do provide the necessary framework you need to get a handle on your schedule and begin to line it up with becoming the person you want to be.

G is for goals

I'm sure you have read enough books or magazine articles, attended meetings at work, or watched enough late-night infomercials to know that goals are necessary if you are going to accomplish much. You also know that goals should be specific—with a beginning point, an ending point, and markers along the way that help you know whether you are on the right track. Goals are to-do statements. They are action points to something you are going to accomplish.

Let's say one of my purpose statements is "I want to become a better father." What does it mean to become a better father? Goals will help add some focus and clarity to that purpose statement. To be a better father, there are some things I need to do. Here are some goal statements, then, to go along with my purpose statement:

- Beginning on October 12 (or perhaps the end of football season!) and for three months, I am going to spend Monday nights from six to nine o'clock doing something with my daughter that she wants to do (besides watching television).
- In January I will take my sons with me on a two-day ski trip.
- Each morning I will spend ten minutes praying for each of my children about something specific going on in their lives.

I can answer yes or no to the question "Did I spend Monday evenings with my daughter from six to nine o'clock doing something that she likes?" Goal statements provide a road map for the general direction you want to go, in line with your purposes. It's like saying "I am going west, and I am taking Route 66 to get there." Goals give you a way to measure the progress of your purpose.

A is for activities

Here is where we get down to brass tacks. Make a list of all the things you are doing, and then ask yourself "Am I doing what I said I wanted to do to become what I said I wanted to become?"

If not, then ask yourself why. Why are you doing things that don't help you become the kind of person you want to become? What is hindering that? Now there are, of course, things you don't want to do that you have to do. One such item on my list is taking out the trash. But if your list of activities is flooded with things that don't help you become the person you want to be, it's possible that you don't really want to become that person after all. Or consider this: you may not be willing to make the choices necessary to do what you need to do to become what you want to be.

> *Why are you doing things that don't help you become the kind of person you want to become?*

I am not going to try and convince you that P–G–A is an easy exercise or that you will suddenly stop being so busy. I *am* going to suggest that if you will be among the few who choose to work through the P–G–A formula, write it down, and review it regularly—you *will* use your slice of time to be busy with what matters most to you. And if that happens, perhaps you will no longer feel too busy.

A time for everything

After reflecting on life and its consequences, King Solomon wrote out on a scroll a small treatise about time from God's point of view. The words are as instructive for us today as they were for him more than three thousand years ago. "There is a time for everything, and a season for every activity under heaven" (Ecclesiastes 3:1).

Did you catch that? "A time for everything, and a season for every activity," every activity in its "season." We all have different seasons or stages of life—being single, being newly married, raising preschoolers, raising middle schoolers, launching a new business, putting the kids through college, being empty-nesters, being grandparents. . . . Add to this the complication of military service, blending families, or starting a family later in life, and there will be more stress in the area of time.

God always provides enough time to do his will—that which he wants us to do. You can do everything God wants you to do . . . just not all at the same time or in the same season. And that's the key.

Most activities are not right or wrong but often are time appropriate. It's hard to balance a vigorous television schedule of sporting events, drastically improve your golf game, travel extensively with your work, have a vibrant relationship with your spouse, and be a responsible and loving parent to your preteen kids all at the same time. Even if you are one of those exceptional individuals who has a seemingly endless supply of energy for everyone and everything, you are probably driving the rest of your family crazy. (And most likely you didn't even read this sentence because you are skimming the book, just picking up the main ideas.)

There is only a season of attending college. There is only one first year of a marriage during which its foundation can be built. There is only a season when you can snuggle with your kids and read them stories before they go to bed. There is only a season of throwing yourself into your dream job. There is only a season when you can put a lost tooth under your kid's pillow with the shared expectancy of a dollar being there in the morning. There is only one season when you can teach your kids to throw and catch a baseball. There is only a season of riding roller coasters with the youth group. There are only so many recitals and games that you can attend and become your child's biggest fan. There are only so many Saturday afternoons you have to build memories before another season comes along.

How we handle the earlier seasons determines the level of enjoyment of the later seasons of life. Both of my (Eric's) parents are retired and in their eighties. They are active and in great health. One day my sister asked them how they fill their days now that they are retired. My dad smiled and answered, "Oh, we review a lot." One day we will look at the snapshots of our lives—shared joys and sorrows, laughter and tears, times around the table, first dates, leaving home, family celebrations, fun with friends, vacations. God will give us time for them all if we take them in their seasons.

> *Before you say yes to a new commitment, first determine what you will then have to say no to.*

Scrap and simplify

Stress often comes when we already have too much on our plates and keep adding more. Living in "seasons" grants us permission to scrap something before we add something. Allow me to illustrate with Larry's story.

When Larry got married in his early thirties, he assumed that when he joined households with his bride, he would bring all of his belongings. Being single had given Larry the luxury of adding things to his life without subtracting anything. So he had two sets of golf clubs, nearly forty ties, and dozens of shirts, sport coats, and pants that he had accumulated since his college years. He was always adding and never subtracting.

Pam had other ideas. Before they joined their households, Larry had to decide the optimum number (not the maximum number) of items to fit the limited space. Once that number was set (say three pairs of jeans, five pairs of slacks, twelve shirts, and twelve neckties), then every time Larry got a new necktie for Christmas, before he added that tie to his wardrobe, he had to decide which tie he was going to get rid of. If he wanted to buy a new shirt, he had to determine if this new shirt was better than the worst shirt in his closet because that one was about to be tossed out or given away.

Larry and his wife discovered the principle of simplicity that can be applied to activities as well as to articles of clothing. Before you say yes to a new commitment, first determine what you will then have to say no to. For instance, you probably have to say no to playing in an adult softball league if you are going to have time to coach your son or daughter's Little League team.

Say yes better

I (Rick) couldn't begin to count the number of times I've been told to just say no. Of course, I usually hear that after I catch myself being in over my head and looking for ways not to be so busy. At management seminars, from friends, and in books the message is, learn to say no better. But maybe that's the wrong message.

What I have learned is that for each yes I have spoken, I have silently spoken a number of no's. For example, if I say yes to a project or program that has me in meetings one night a week, I am automatically saying no to my family that night, I am saying no to other priorities or projects I have on my plate, and I am saying no to personal time. My one yes produces a whole lot of no's. So the truth is that I am good at saying no. I don't need to learn to say no better. I say no quite a bit, and I bet you do as well. Maybe before we say yes, we should first contemplate all of the things we are saying no to.

TEMPORAL LIFE VS. ETERNITY

Imagine Jesus, existing from the beginning to the end of all eternity, stepping into time and into your life. He wants to give you some good advice. He says, "Do not work for food that spoils, but for food that endures to eternal life" (John 6:27) and, "Do not store up for yourselves treasures on earth, where moth and rust destroy, and where thieves break in and steal. But store up for yourselves treasures in heaven, where moth and rust do not destroy, and where thieves do not break in and steal" (Matthew 6:19, 20).

> *To invest in eternity means you need to invest your time in developing the inner man more than the outer man.*

Paul gives his view on perspective as well. Read his words thoughtfully: "We do not lose heart. Though outwardly we are wasting away, yet inwardly we are being renewed day by day. For our light and momentary troubles are achieving for us an eternal glory that far outweighs them all" (2 Corinthians 4:16, 17).

To invest in eternity means you need to invest your time in developing what Paul indicates as the *inner* man more than the *outer* man. Two things are happening simultaneously. First, the outer man is wasting away (although sometimes it appears to be getting larger). Here's some pretty depressing news. At about age thirty, the body no longer gets better. Rather, there is a slow process of decline that is taking place. The process can be postponed but not avoided altogether.

In 1975 four of the oldest actors who starred as Tarzan gathered to celebrate the centennial birthday of Edgar Rice Burroughs, author of the twenty-six books about Tarzan. Oldest among them was seventy-one-year-old Olympic swimming champion Johnny Weismuller. Joining Johnny was another Olympian, Buster Crabb, along with two other lesser-known Tarzans.[7] Posing with their outfits on, it was clear that the sands of time had shifted. If any of the actors had dropped a few pounds, the pounds dropped from their chests into their waistlines.

Fitness guru Jack La Lanne performed many famous publicity stunts over the years, including doing 1,033 push-ups in twenty-three minutes. On his seventieth birthday, he towed seventy boats carrying seventy people while swimming handcuffed and shackled in the Pacific Ocean off Long Beach, California.[8] Jack followed a strict diet and worked out every day of his life since 1926. Although he lived well into his nineties, eventually he too succumbed to the outer man's wasting away.

What's the point? Advertising will tell you that this life is all there is. The ads for cross trainers, ab-flexors, rowing machines, stair climbers, and giant rubber balls have brainwashed us into thinking this body has ultimate importance. We want to dress it up, bulk it up, shape it up, and slim it down. We can and should make short-term investments in the outer man, but the outer man is wasting away. There is another investment to be made—and that is in the *inner* man.

The you that lasts

The *inner* man is the real you—the part that thinks, reasons, feels, and wills. It is the part of you that reflects the character of Jesus. It's the you that will go to Heaven and spend eternity with God. What did the 2 Corinthians 4 passage say? While the outer man is wasting away, a second thing is happening: "inwardly we are being renewed day by day." While we tend to major on developing the outer, God has committed himself to the inner man. Do you need to be concerned about your outer body—your fitness and your looks? Of course you do, as part of your stewardship. But if you have to choose between developing one or the other, focus on what will last—on what will be the best investment in your future.

How can you cooperate with God and develop the inner self? Allow the circumstances of life to shape and transform your character. The second part of that passage explains, "For our light and momentary troubles are achieving for us an eternal glory that far outweighs them all." What was Paul referring to when he wrote about "light and momentary troubles"? Here's some more from Paul to shed a bit of light.

> I have . . . been in prison more frequently, been flogged more severely, and been exposed to death again and again. Five times I received . . . forty lashes minus one. Three times I was beaten with rods, once I was stoned, three times I was shipwrecked, I spent a night and a day in the open sea, I have been constantly on the move. I have been in danger from rivers, in danger from bandits, in danger from my own countrymen, in danger from Gentiles; in danger in the city, in danger in the country, in danger at sea; and in danger from false brothers (2 Corinthians 11:23-26).

What does God want from you? He wants it all—your talents and skills, your possessions, your experiences, your influence, and your time. But he provides it all!

Your trials are probably a far cry from Paul's, but they are real nonetheless. Health problems, relational estrangement, job loss, death, illness of a loved one, and depression are all very real and painful. Your question shouldn't be "Why did God allow this?" but rather "How can God use this in my life to make me more like the person he wants me to be?"

You can't always choose what happens to you, but you can choose how you respond to the curveballs life throws your way. Viktor Frankl survived a Nazi concentration camp and emerged to write *Man's Search for Meaning* in 1946. He noted that the difference between those who willed to live and those who chose to die was attitude. "Everything can be taken from a man but one thing: the last of the human freedoms—to choose one's attitude in any given set of circumstances, to choose one's own way."[9]

God wants to remind you that trials are not an interruption to his plan but are a way to develop your inner self.

Giving back to God

What does God want from you? He wants it all. Does that seem like a lot to ask? Yes, it is! But remember that he gave it all—and look at the return you'll get when you invest it back with him. You are invited to be in the eternal story God is writing and quite possibly catch a small glimpse of Heaven on earth too.

When Moses lived in Egypt, he had it all—he was like royalty. Then he lost it all because he got angry and killed a man. And then, when he was finally living an uneventful, calm, and content life in a foreign land, God asked him to step outside of his comfort zone and step into God's story. God called from a burning bush and asked Moses to invest it all and lead the Israelites out of slavery in Egypt. God asked Moses, with his past, his pain, and now his contentment, to be the spokesperson for one of God's eternal purposes. Moses made excuse after excuse as to why he wasn't the right person to be a part of the story. Finally, God had heard enough of the excuses and told Moses to tell the people that "I AM has sent me to you!" (Exodus 3:14).

What does God want from you? He wants it all—your talents and skills, your possessions, your experiences, your influence, and your time. But he provides it all! God said to Moses and is saying to you and me, "I AM is all you need." Like Moses, I can think of plenty of reasons why I cannot or should not get involved.

- I am not wise enough—but God says, "I AM"
- I am not confident in myself—"I AM"

- I am not sure of the answers—"I AM"
- I am uncertain of the future—"I AM"
- I am not strong enough—"I AM"
- I am not over my past—"I AM"
- I am not capable—"I AM"
- I am not sure of the story—"I AM"

God can use you to make an eternal difference in the world. He can help you to make each moment count forever. God can and will help you become who he needs you to be when you decide to step into what he is doing in the world. He's given you a slice of eternity. What's your response?

WHAT ABOUT YOU?

1. How can you create greater margins of time in your life?

2. What should you stop doing that currently is not adding any value to your life or the lives of others?

3. Have you ever taken the time to define and evaluate your purposes, goals, and accompanying activities? If not, why not do it today?

4. What can you do to invest today in your inner self, the real you?

5. How can you use your talents and skills, possessions, experiences, influence, and time to further God's eternal purposes?

10
ETERNITY IN OUR HEARTS

Millions long for immortality who do not know what to do
with themselves on a rainy Sunday afternoon.

—SUSAN ERTZ

I f you enjoy watching college football on Saturday afternoons or catching an NFL game on Sundays, one thing you will always see is the head coach wearing a headset. Most likely he's not talking to his wife or kids or arranging for after-game snacks. He's connected to and getting insight from one or more coaches in the press box—people who can see more than he can. No football coach worth his salt would try to coach his team without his eye in the sky. The perspective from above allows him to understand the bigger patterns that are playing out on the field.

PERSPECTIVE

Perspective is the vantage point from which we view something. It helps us make wise decisions. Perspective does not change the facts, but it certainly adds to them.

Jerry worked his way through college serving as a waiter in a Chinese restaurant. One customer in particular was the bane of every waiter and waitress's existence. She was an elderly woman who came in every day for lunch. No matter how good the service or the meal was, she would reach into her pocketbook, pull out a penny, and place it on the table as a tip. The waiters and waitresses were cordial to her face, but when they returned to the kitchen, they were cursing and throwing the pennies against the wall in disgust.

Because Jerry was known as a Christian, the crew made sure he was assigned to her table whenever they could manage it. One day Jerry got up the nerve to talk to this woman, and eventually he asked her why she tipped only one penny, pointing out how waiters and waitresses hated to serve her table. She answered by asking, "Have you ever looked at one of these pennies to see what they are worth?"

At his first opportunity, Jerry ran down to a local coin shop to have his penny appraised. Much to his surprise, his penny was worth two hundred dollars! Returning to the restaurant, he told his coworkers the good news. Soon they were all on their hands and knees, looking behind every appliance and cleaning every drain in search of the discarded pennies they had flung. The employees had a new perspective. What was once seen as worthless became extremely valuable. That's what perspective does—perspective spotlights value.

But there is another perspective that is even more important—the perspective of time. What is it that you do today that will still be valuable to you five years from now . . . twenty years from now . . . fifty years from now . . . a thousand years from now? What does your life look like from the perspective of eternity?

You have a date of birth, and eventually there will be a date that marks your death, but is that your life—simply the counting and calendaring of the days, weeks, and months between the date of your birth and the date of your death? On every gravestone there are two dates, but there is a dash between the two. The following anonymous poem describes the significance of that dash.

The Dash Between the Dates

Graveside services were over now.
Everyone had left and I was alone.
I began to read the names and dates
Chiseled here and there on every stone.

The name showed whether it was Mom or Dad,
Or daughter or baby son.
The dates were different, the amount the same,
There were two dates on every one.

It was then that I noticed something
Just a simple line.
It was the dash between the dates,
And placed there, it stood for time.

All at once it dawned on me,
How important that little line!
The dates placed there belong to God,
But the line is yours and mine.

. . . .

We know He's written the first date down
Of each and every one;
And we're sure the hands will write again,
For the last date has to come.

The hands will write the last date down
Quite soon, perhaps, for some;
But upon the line between my dates and yours,
I trust He'd write, "Well done, well done!"[1]

The dash—your life—really is a piling up of a multitude of moments, isn't it? What matters is what you choose to do with those moments. All our lives are significantly more than calendars filled with accomplishments or failures. A calendar simply records or plans activity, marking time.

Looking back on your life from the viewpoint of eternity, what will seem like a good investment?

Often the world defines people by accomplishments, successes, or lack of them. It's possible you have been invited onto someone's Who's Who list, but more than likely you are in the 99 percent of people in the world who will never see their names on a list like that. More than a name on a list or a birthday on a calendar, your life is a story being written. Moment by moment and choice after choice, you are writing a story. And the real question to be answered in this story is, Whose "who" are you?

Living for the dot or living for the line?

The dash in the above poem is a line that represents your life. But in the introduction of this book, we talked about another line. Remember the long line of eternity? It's been several years since I (Eric) first heard a speaker use that illustration in talking about eternal perspective. He drew the line across a classroom-size chalkboard. He told us that the line represented eternity and that it has no beginning or end. I remember how he ever so carefully used the chalk to press a small dot into the line. After he explained that the dot represented the short span of one person's life inside this very long eternity, he gave us his zinger of a challenge: "Are you living for the dot, or are you living for the line?" Wow! What a question!

What if somehow you were able to step back into time and found yourself in the year 1985 . . . and here is the good part—you knew everything you know now. What would you invest in, knowing what you know now? How about a little company founded by Paul Allen and Bill Gates called Microsoft? Offered to the public at twenty-one dollars per share, accounting for several stock splits, one share would now be worth approximately three hundred shares. That means one share would be worth around six thousand three hundred dollars today! If you had bought just one hundred shares (for two thousand one hundred dollars), you would now be a millionaire several times over.

Do you see what tremendous insight the perspective of time affords you? Looking back, you can see what would have been a good invest-ment. Good investments are those that are valuable when you cash them in. Looking back on your life from the viewpoint of eternity, what will seem like a good investment?

Moses and eternal perspective

Moses serves as a stellar example of one who lived from an eternal perspective—captured and captivated by the unseen and eternal more than by the visible and temporary. The Bible says that Moses believed "it was better to suffer for the sake of the Messiah than to own the treasures of Egypt, for he was looking ahead to the great reward that God would give him. It was by faith that Moses left the land of Egypt. He was not afraid of the king. Moses kept right on going because he kept his eyes on the one who is invisible" (Hebrews 11:26, 27, *NLT*).

Moses was motivated by an unseen future and by an unseen God, yet to him the unseen was more powerful than the seen.

One of the disciples who had sat at Jesus' feet, soaking in his words, wrote, "The day of the Lord will come like a thief, in which the heavens will pass away with a roar and the elements will be destroyed with intense heat, and the earth and its works will be burned up" (2 Peter 3:10, *NASB*). One day your house, your car, your collections, and your photos will all go up in smoke, along with the earth. What will last are the unseen, eternal things.

When I (Eric) was about eight years old, I was somewhat enamored by fire. Back in the 1950s it was still permissible to burn combustible trash, and we had for that purpose a large barrel perforated with holes. Regularly, when my dad threw cardboard boxes into the barrel, I pretended they were little houses burning up.

One day I was on my front porch with a large cardboard box when my across-the-street neighbor, Diane Farrell, stood on the bottom stair and asked me what I was doing. "I'm making a house." Well, she got all excited and ran home, quickly returning with scissors, cloth, and crayons. What we built together was a thing of beauty. I cut windows into the box, and Diane made the curtains for those windows. She colored the door red and made the roof of forest green shingles. I suppose she thought we were playing house or something, but I had different plans. After constructing our house, I carried it out back, placed it on top of the trash-burning barrel, and lit a match to it. It was a delight to see the flames licking the sides of the house and curling out the windows. I loved seeing the first flames break through the roof before all of it was consumed and reduced to ashes. As I enjoyed the incineration, Diane ran home crying.

Here is my point: if Diane had known that all her work was going to be burned up, she probably would not have invested so much time and effort in building a house that wouldn't last.

INVESTING IN WHAT LASTS

I hope you enjoy your house, your car, and all of the other things you have, but having an eternal perspective means you don't build your life around them. If the earth and its entire works are going to be consumed by fire one day, is there anything that will survive the fire? What can you invest in that is fireproof? The Bible suggests three things that last forever.

Your relationship with God

First of all, you can invest in your relationship with God. In one of Jesus' prayers, he slipped in a definition of eternal life. He prayed, "Now this is eternal life: that they may know you, the only true God, and Jesus Christ, whom you have sent" (John 17:3).

Eternal life is not merely life defined by a *quantity* of existence that lasts forever but also by a *quality* of relationship—knowing God and Jesus. The Old Testament prophet Jeremiah penned these words: "Thus says the LORD, 'Let not a wise man boast of his wisdom, and let not the mighty man boast of his might, let not a rich man boast of his riches; but let him who boasts boast of this, that he understands and knows Me, that I am the LORD who exercises lovingkindness, justice, and righteousness on earth; for I delight in these things,' declares the LORD" (Jeremiah 9:23, 24, *NASB*).

God says not to boast about, or find your identity in, things like wisdom—how smart you think you are or what degrees you might have. Don't find your identity in your might—either in physical prowess or power of position over people. Don't find your identity in your wealth—how much you possess. These are the calling cards of those who don't know God—boasting of intelligence, power, and money. But God has a different plan. He says, "Find your identity in the fact that you know and understand me!" He wants us to know beyond a shadow of a doubt that he is the one who exercises lovingkindness (every good thing), justice (every fair thing), and righteousness (every right thing) on earth. He alone (not our intelligence, power, or money) can provide every good, fair, and right thing in our lives.

How do you get to know someone? Through two-way communication. Communicate with God through honest and candid prayer, both speaking to and listening to him. God communicates to you through his Word; you get to know God by learning about his character and attributes described there.

The writers of the psalms describe God in terms we can understand and respond to.

For many years as I've read the Bible, I have taken note of the words that describe God. Theologians like to use big words like *omnipotent, omnipresent,* and *omniscient* to describe the nature of God. While these are accurate descriptions, the writers of the Bible—especially the writers of the psalms—used more down-to-earth words. They describe God in terms we can understand and respond to. In Psalm 27 David writes, "The LORD is my light and my salvation; whom shall I fear? The LORD is the defense of my life; whom shall I dread?" (vv. 1, 2, *NASB*).

Or how about this one from Psalm 23? "The LORD is my shepherd, I shall not want" (v. 1, *NASB*).

Or this one from Psalm 46? "God is our refuge and strength, a very present help in trouble. Therefore we will not fear, though the earth should change, and though the mountains slip into the heart of the sea; though its waters roar and foam, though the mountains quake at its swelling pride" (vv. 1-3, *NASB*).

In each example above, the writer filled in his personal response to what he knew of the character of God. But when one of God's attributes is given without the response, you can fill in your own response. Here are a couple of examples:

- Psalm 2:6—God is my king. "Lord, because you are king, I am not king. I willfully choose today to submit to you in all I do."
- Psalm 3:3—God is a shield around me. "Lord, be my shield . . . my protector today. Guard me from anything that would destroy my walk with you or keep me from following you."

Writers of the Bible used countless words to refer to God— words like *powerful, graceful, merciful,* and *love.* The Bible also calls God my strong tower, my rock, my help, my father, my hope, my confidence, my strong refuge, my sun and my shield, and my dwelling place. Each of these emotive words elicits a response from our hearts. The late A. W. Tozer wrote, "What comes into our minds when we think about God is the most important thing about us."[2] So one of the best ways to invest in what lasts is to get to know the God of the Bible.

You get to know people over time by doing things together. You also get to know God by inviting him into every area, facet, and aspect of your life—your home life, work life, hobbies, and recreation.

Several years ago pastor Robert Boyd Munger wrote a little booklet entitled *My Heart, Christ's Home,* building on Ephesians 3:17, "I pray that Christ will be more and more at home in your hearts as you trust in him" (*NLT*). Munger compares inviting Christ into your life to inviting him into your home. Because Jesus is not content to stand by the entrance, he asks permission, room by room, to dwell in each of those also.

The first room he wants to enter is the study, which represents the mind; then the dining room with your appetites and desires; then the living room where you meet with Jesus on a daily basis; then the workroom representing your talents, strengths, and skills; and then the recreation room representing your friendships, activities, and amusements. The last room is the tiny closet representing those dark areas of your life that you don't want to turn over to Christ because of shame or secret pleasure. But Jesus also wants the key to that room. He is more than capable of cleaning it out.

The booklet ends by transferring the title of the house to Jesus. This is a wonderful illustration of what it means to have every area of your life under the supervision and direction of Jesus.

The following personal statement would be a good pattern for living your life on loan: yield everything I know about myself to everything I know about God.

Incorporating that statement as a lifestyle works both for a brand-new Christ-follower and also for one who has been walking with the Lord for many years. How about you? Have you given Jesus access to every area of your life, your heart, and your home? There is no greater adventure we can have than fully yielding ourselves to God—because our relationship with him will last forever.

God's Word

A study of the Bible will reveal something else that lasts forever—God's Word. Here's what Isaiah says about the Bible: "The grass withers and the flowers fall, but the word of our God stands forever" (Isaiah 40:8). Every time you see your lawn wilting on a hot day, or anytime you see flower petals gathering beneath a vase on the kitchen table, it is in contrast to God's Word, which lasts for eternity. God's unchanging Word is something you can bank on.

There are many good plans to get you into God's Word. One is to read through the Bible every year or so. Billy Graham reads from Psalms and Proverbs every day. He says that the psalms teach us how to get along with God and the proverbs teach us how to get along with people.

Some people can work out their own plan. For most people, though, reading the Bible can feel like picking up a book written in a foreign language. It's helpful to have some sort of guide. Learning and understanding the Bible can sometimes happen best in community. Are you in a small group study with others? Learning in a group environment encourages dialogue and real-life application as well as personal study. Many small groups also take their faith on the road. We have known many small groups that are not only Bible studies but also service groups.

Consider, for example, this story. A number of businessmen (some retired, some still active in business) had discovered together that a small group provided a place for growing friendships with others who also desired to grow in their faith. They had been meeting for Bible study, prayer, and conversation for years. One particular Bible study on the heels of Hurricane Katrina was about service. As an action step, the group was invited to share in a community service opportunity that involved canvassing their neighborhoods with resealable bags, asking their neighbors to fill the bags with various necessities that would be sent on to help victims of the Katrina disaster.

One of the men in the group, Randy, said, "I was attracted to the group because there was a commitment to loving God and loving people. I have to admit that because of my busy life, serving people has not always come easy for me. It's hard for many men to reach out beyond their work life and family life. This particular Bible study on service was where the rubber would meet the road for me."

It was a different kind of experience for these highly successful businessmen to be going door-to-door with little resealable bags. Randy continues, "Most of us who volunteered went forward with fear and trepidation. It certainly was not our favorite pastime to go door-to-door asking people for help. Some of our neighbors answered their doors with angst and concern. Nonetheless, many people took our little bags. If no one was home at a particular house, we hung the bags with an instruction sheet on their doors and committed ourselves to coming back and picking up the filled bags the next week. That's when the fun really began. We were pleasantly surprised to discover how many of our neighbors had actually gone out and purchased items, filled the bags, and had them ready for our pickup."

It's better to be ankle-deep in application than neck-deep in knowledge.

Upon returning to pick up the bags, the men found that some of their neighbors had some very interesting stories to share. One lady came to the door with several bags filled to the brim. She had taken the initial bag and filled it, then added several more of her own. She admitted that when one of the men knocked on her door the week before and told his story, she was somewhat taken back because, for various reasons, she had not had a very positive impression of churches. But after reviewing the instruction sheet within the bag, she concluded that any church that supported the Katrina victims with this kind of effort could not be all bad. As a result, she started asking questions about the church.

When we serve we have the opportunity to extend grace in many small ways. We are living out the eternal truths found in the Bible. You never know how an act of service might touch another person, how you might help someone else find grace at the intersections.

No matter what plan you have to get into God's Word, it's not about how much you know, but how you live as a result of what you are learning. It's better to be ankle-deep in application than neck-deep in knowledge. It is interesting that, as far as we can tell, every time Jesus talked about the Word of God, he talked in terms of application and not knowledge.

After delivering the Sermon on the Mount (Matthew 5–7), Jesus concluded by telling about two different responses to what he taught.

> Everyone who hears these words of mine and puts them into practice is like a wise man who built his house on the rock. The rain came down, the streams rose, and the winds blew and beat against that house; yet it did not fall, because it had its foundation on the rock. But everyone who hears these words of mine and does not put them into practice is like a foolish man who built his house on sand. The rain came down, the streams rose, and the winds blew and beat against that house, and it fell with a great crash (Matthew 7:24-27).

It's pretty easy to see the contrast. Both men had the same basic situation, like two people sitting side by side in church listening to a sermon . . . two people hearing the same content in a small group . . . two people reading their Bibles together. They both heard and read the same things. As long as the weather was sunny and dry, it was difficult to differentiate between the two houses. But when the rains came and the winds blew and the river rose, one house stood and the other fell. It was the "putting into practice" that made the difference.

In 1991 I (Eric) spent the summer in Mexico City with my family. The city still showed the marks of the devastating earthquake that rocked Mexico City on September 19, 1985, when hundreds of buildings collapsed, thousands of people died, and two hundred fifty thousand were left homeless. Interestingly, the buildings from the Aztec and colonial periods stood strong; it was the buildings constructed in the last forty years that pancaked under the force of the 8.1 quake.

With such devastation, it was assumed that Mexico must have shoddy building codes, but further investigation showed that Mexico City had building codes equal to those of any major city of the world.

The building codes were solid. What was not solid was the application of those codes. They were not "put into practice." In many cases, the reinforcing steel used in cement construction was not welded together, as the code required, but simply *wired* together.

It is application of the code, not just having the code, that makes all the difference. The apostle James writes,

> Do not merely listen to the word, and so deceive yourselves. Do what it says. Anyone who listens to the word but does not do what it says is like a man who looks at his face in a mirror and, after looking at himself, goes away and immediately forgets what he looks like. But the man who looks intently into the perfect law that gives freedom, and continues to do this, not forgetting what he has heard, but doing it—he will be blessed in what he does (James 1:22-25).

The deception that James writes about is the deception that substitutes knowledge for action and hearing for doing.

Why do we look in a mirror? Remember the TV show *Happy Days*? The Fonz (Henry Winkler) would often look in the mirror and think about running a comb through his hair, but then, implying that one couldn't improve on perfection, he walked away.

The rest of us mere mortals look in the mirror to make corrections—comb our hair, put on makeup, shave. The mirror tells us what we look like and how we can make improvements . . . but it is important that we actually respond to what the mirror says and make the corrections. This is the essence of what needs to happen with Bible input—hearing, reading, studying, or discussing. We need to act on what it says. Here's how a couple of friends of ours are putting into practice what the Bible is telling them.

A few months ago a couple of young professionals asked a friend of mine (Eric's) if they could get together to learn how to study the Bible.

They were obviously hungry to learn and grow. But Don told them, "I'll teach you how to study the Bible, but I want to make it very practical." Soon this newly formed small group found themselves hanging six doors for a mom with two disabled teenage sons. "This is what we need to be doing much more frequently," was the response—a little less talk and a lot more action.

Jon is a vice president of a Colorado title company; he's also a small-group leader. Jon's group has learned firsthand the value and power of learning God's Word and serving others. "We were studying *Love Each Other* by John Ortberg," says Jon. "At the end of the first session, there is a section called 'Serving and Being Served,' and it challenged us to show someone the love that God shows us."

Have you ever thought about the fact that people last forever— either in relationship with God or estranged from his presence?

So how did they put God's Word into action? After brainstorming what kind of project they could do together, one woman spoke up and shared that she knew an individual with multiple sclerosis (MS) who needed some help. The group agreed on a date and went to the house. The ladies cleaned the inside, and the guys cleaned the outside.

Jon sums it up: "Serving with these people and living life with them (camping, cookouts, and movies) has brought us closer as a small group, and God's Word comes alive when we serve together."

People

Have you ever thought about the fact that people last forever— either in relationship with God or estranged from his presence (see

2 Thessalonians 1:9)? Investing in the lives of people is probably the most powerful investment you can make.

A friend of mine once asked me, "How many seeds are in an apple?" I tried to think back to my high school biology class and remember the traits of monocots and dicots and whether the seed number was odd or even, but in the end I suggested we cut open an apple and count the seeds. But the bigger question is, how many apples are in a seed? Whoa! Now that's a *big* question, because it has to do with potential. There are innumerable apples in each seed.

John Wooden is the most successful college basketball coach of all time. At UCLA he never had a losing season, and he won ten national championships in twelve years. His eighty-eight game winning streak is probably beyond the reach of any basketball team of the modern era. More than a coach, Wooden was a mentor to his players. The accolades for the marks he left on his men continue to pour in from grateful players and their families. Interviews with Wooden are full of bits of wisdom from his father and a few of his mentors. He loved quoting verbatim a poem by a teacher—that could very well have been his own description of coaching.

They Ask Me Why I Teach
by Glennice Harmon

They ask me why I teach
And I reply, "Where could I find more splendid company?"
There sits a statesman,
Strong, unbiased, wise,
Another later Webster
Silver-tongued.
And there a doctor
Whose quick, steady hand

Can mend a bone or stem the lifeblood's flow.
A builder sits beside him—
Upward rise the arches of that church he builds wherein
That minister will speak the word of God,
And lead a stumbling soul to touch the Christ.

And, all about
A lesser gathering
Of farmers, merchants, teachers,
Laborers, men
Who work and vote and build
And plan and pray into a great tomorrow.
And, I say,
"I may not see the church,
Or hear the word,
Or eat the food their hands will grow."
And yet—I may.
And later I may say,
"I knew the lad, And he was strong,
Or weak, or kind, or proud
Or bold or gay.
I knew him once,
But then he was a boy."
They ask me why I teach and I reply,
"Where could I find more splendid company?"[3]

Wooden understood the eternal potential of one person's impact on others.

Remember that touching scene at the end of the movie *Mr. Holland's Opus*? Based on a true story, the movie features Mr. Holland, a music teacher who taught at the same high school for thirty years. When funding for school music programs was eliminated, Mr. Holland decided it was time to retire. After he boxed up his things from his desk and took one last look at the music room, he heard a commotion coming from the auditorium. With his wife and son by his side, he walked into an auditorium filled with friends and former students who were there to say their farewells. The state's lieutenant governor, a former student of Mr. Holland's, acted as the master of ceremonies. Before she took her seat (along with the orchestra members from the past thirty years) to play Mr. Holland's original score, she told Mr. Holland that these former students were really his greatest work—his opus—because he left his mark on every one of them. To give ourselves away to people is an investment in eternity.

To give ourselves away to people is an investment in eternity.

You probably don't know the name Mordecai Ham. He sounds like a character from a fictional work, but he isn't. He was the man who led fifteen-year-old Billy Graham to faith in Christ in 1934. Billy is a seed that has produced millions of apples. When you invest your life helping people into Heaven, you have invested in eternity. Isn't it interesting that Jesus, who evaluated carefully how he spent his every moment, had time for children? Maybe he understood something about potential . . . about seeds in an apple. What will your opus be? Where are you planting your seeds?

ETERNITY IN YOUR HEART

Every one of us is going to die. Psalm 49 says, "All can see that wise men die; the foolish and the senseless alike perish and leave their wealth to others. Their tombs will remain their houses forever, their dwellings for endless generations, though they had named lands after themselves. But man, despite his riches, does not endure; he is like the beasts that perish" (vv. 10-12). Even though we know we are going to die, everybody instinctively wants to leave some type of lasting legacy. It is part of the way God designed each of us. God "set eternity in the hearts of men" (Ecclesiastes 3:11). Each person longs to leave his or her mark, albeit small, on the world.

Lands or buildings named after someone may last a long time. (Think of Pennsylvania, named after William Penn, or the Washington Monument, named after George Washington.) But time is very short compared to eternity. The way to invest in eternity is to invest in things that really last—your relationship with God, the Word of God, and people.

Living with one foot raised

In 1540, forty-nine-year-old Ignatius Loyola founded the Jesuit order. In 1540 there were ten Jesuits. By 1556, the year of Loyola's death, there were one thousand Jesuits. And by 1580 there were five thousand Jesuits. The Jesuits cut a huge swath across the globe, founding thirty colleges in their first twelve years of existence and two hundred colleges in the first sixty years. They eventually founded so many secondary schools and universities that by the mid-eighteenth century, one out of every five Europeans was educated in a Jesuit school.[4] They crossed mountains, forged through rivers, and filled in many of the white spaces on the maps. They were the confidants and advisers to European kings, Indian moguls, and Chinese emperors.

Vladimir Lenin envied the dedication of the Jesuits and once said, sighing, that with only a dozen cadres as talented and dedicated as the Jesuits, his Communist movement would sweep the world.[5]

The Jesuits' working motto was the Latin word *magis,* or "more," which suggested the idea of always striving for something more, something greater. Loyola often described the ideal Jesuit as "living with one foot raised"[6]—always ready to respond to emerging opportunities by taking the next step. They were ready to go to any place on the globe with a mere forty-eight hours' notice, to fulfill their mission: "to preach, hear confessions, and use all other means [they could] . . . to help souls."[7] Wouldn't Living with One Foot Raised make a fitting motto for us in these times?

> *God is the God of second chances and multiple opportunities.*

The best is yet to come

No matter what age you are, you can know that your best years are still ahead. God is the God of second chances and multiple opportunities. We get lots of do-overs to help shape the endings of our own stories. Have you discovered your way to impact eternity? Is it big enough to capture your attention and devotion? It's been said, "You start dying when you have nothing to live for, and you start living when you have something to die for." Do you have a purpose worth giving your life to?

My friend Roger Hershey is passionate about eternal perspective. For over thirty years he has worked in campus ministry—leading young men to Christ, discipling them toward Christian maturity, and sending them off into the world to lead others. There are few people I know who have affected eternity like Roger.

When Roger speaks to college students about where they will invest their lives and time, he is so excited that, by his own admission, he almost hemorrhages. Speaking on eternal perspective is his favorite topic! He closes his talks by retelling the story of a dream he once had.

Our house sits at the end of a cul-de-sac, and in my dream, I am awakened from my sleep by a loud, thunderous noise on the street. Without awakening my wife, I hurriedly get dressed and rush downstairs. I pause, then open the front door to see what all the commotion is about.

There in front of me is an army of mounted riders, dressed in white . . . their white stallions pawing the ground and snorting. Walking toward the curb, I look closely into the faces of the riders. There is Tom, whom I led to Christ and discipled when we were students at Penn State thirty years ago, and there's Bill, whom I shared Christ with at Daytona Beach in the early 1980s, and there's Jim, a fraternity boy who practically lived in our home and was loved into the kingdom. There are Sam and John and Josh and Tim and Aaron and Donny and Raul and Seth and Akbar and Rashid. . . . Why, they're all here . . . the missionaries, the pastors, the doctors, the teachers, and businessmen who all leveraged their lives for the kingdom.

Then my eyes come to the front and center of the riders. It's a strong, kind face that I see. It's the face of Jesus. And beside him stands a bridled, saddled horse. There is no rider on this horse. Jesus is holding the reins. And he looks down on me and with the smile of a father, he hands me the reins and says, "Well done, good and faithful servant. Let's ride!"[8]

Revelation 19 talks about the rider on the white horse accompanied by other riders—the faithful followers of Christ. On that day when we step into eternity, all believers can expect to ride side by side with the

Lord. Wow! Stop for just a moment and picture that as it might be portrayed in a Steven Spielberg movie. What a victorious scene! And, since we with our human limitations can't begin to imagine the dimensions of all God has planned, the scene will surely be more glorious, more powerful, and more victorious than any image we can conjure up.

At times when life gets us down, it would be wise to pull back and remind ourselves of eternity.

Now, let's go back to the other aspect of Roger's dream. He pictured, riding alongside, many people he had influenced for Christ. Who of your family, friends, or coworkers can you picture (or would you like to picture) thundering into eternity with you and King Jesus?

What a great way to keep an eternal perspective and stay focused on how important it is to live your life on loan.

WHAT ABOUT YOU?

1. Are you living for the dot or living for the line? What difference does it make?

2. What "rooms of your home" have you fully yielded to God? What rooms are you holding on to and protecting? Why?

3. What can you do, in a practical way, to invest in eternity by cultivating your relationship with God? spending time in God's Word? giving yourself to others?

4. Can you picture yourself riding victoriously on a horse beside King Jesus? How could that image affect your day-to-day life?

EPILOGUE

Well done, good and faithful servant! You have been faithful

with a few things; I will put you in charge of many things.

Come and share your master's happiness!

—MATTHEW 25:21

Earlier, I (Rick) shared with you a bit about my dad's story. His father changed jobs often, creating a lot of disruption in his home. I suppose that is why my dad took a job with Bristol-Myers at the age of nineteen—and stayed there. He started on a filling line and worked his way up into management. No one else in his family had ever held a job for more than a year or two. He broke old patterns and had hopes for me to go further.

When I told my dad that I was thinking about going into ministry, he nearly had a heart attack. Why would I want to do that? Dad had other plans for me. My decision to go into ministry did not go down easily. "I'm not supporting you for the rest of your life," he said.

Every day my dad made the same drive to the same place; and while his duties changed through the years, giving him some variety, I don't know if I could have done what he did. Then he made the difficult decision to take early retirement after thirty-one years. On the day of my dad's retirement, I arranged to fly home to say thanks—for all he had done, for going to the same place, for breaking an old pattern, for providing, for giving me a leg up, and for demonstrating hard work, loyalty, and perseverance.

Dad didn't know I was coming. I stood outside the same security gate that he had spent three decades going in and out of. I watched him as he came down from his office with a box of things he was bringing home. I could only imagine the mixed emotions he felt—relieved the day was here, sad to leave the place and people he had known for so long, and excited about what was ahead.

As he made his way through the gate, I started to applaud. He looked up to see who was causing all the commotion. When he saw it was me . . . well, it was just one of those moments. A few weeks later my dad wrote to thank me for coming and to express how much that had meant to him. He closed with this: "Someday when this life is over for me here on earth, maybe God will let me be standing at the gate to applaud you on your last day of work and to welcome you home."

Someday you'll draw your last breath. If you have allowed God's story to connect with your story, the Father of the heavens will be standing at the gate to applaud you on your last day of service and to welcome you home. You'll hear God say "Well done!"

A thousand years from now, what about your life will matter? What will make an eternal difference? That's the perspective we challenge you to focus on. As you live this life on loan, pay attention to the intersections, find ways for your story to help others discover God's story. Spend your moments living in God's grace, and you will find the life that is truly life. We guarantee it.

NOTES

Introduction

1. WGBH Educational Foundation, http://main.wgbh.org/imax/shackleton/shackleton.html.

LOVES

1. http://agards-bible-timeline.com/q10_bible-facts.html.

Chapter 2

1. Carl Sandburg. www.dailycelebrations.com/010600.htm.

2. Quotes and information in this account are from a personal interview by the author (Rick).

3. Benjamin Franklin. http://sin.fi.edu/tfi/exhibits/franklin.html.

4. "The Darwin Awards salute the improvement of the human genome by honoring those who remove themselves from it in really stupid ways." www.darwinawards.com.

5. Versions of this account can be found on several Internet sites including www.snopes.com/travel/airline/walters.asp. Larry was charged with several violations from the FAA. Unfortunately, this short-lived fame created a number of difficulties in his life, and Larry chose to take his own life on October 6, 1993.

6. John Gray, *Men Are from Mars, Women Are from Venus* (New York: HarperCollins, 1992), 45.

7. Shaunti Feldhahn, *For Women Only—What You Need to Know About the Inner Lives of Men* (Sisters, Oregon: Multnomah Publishers, 2004), 67–68.

8. Jess McCuan. Paraphrasing information gleaned from *Authentic Happiness* author Martin Seligman and psychology professor Mihaly Csikszentmihalyi, "Successful, Yes, but Still Searching for Happiness," *Inc.* magazine (www.pf.inc.com), March 2005.

Chapter 3

1. G. Jeffrey MacDonald, "Youthful Seekers Try to Find," *USA Today,* April 14, 2005.

2. G. Jeffrey MacDonald, "Youthful Seekers Try to Find."

3. Brennan Manning, *Abba's Child* (Colorado Springs, Colorado: NavPress Publishing Group, 1994), 142.

4. Blaise Pascal. http://en.thinkexist.com/quotation/there_is_a_god_shaped_vacuum_in_the_heart_of/166425.html.

5. Aurelius Augustinus. www.augustinians.org.au/tradition/spirit.html.

6. Read the interview at http://edition.cnn.com/TRANSCRIPTS/0501/07/lkl.01.html.

7. Information in this section from http://across.co.nz/JohnTeshReliefWork.html.

8. Peter Semeyn. Personal conversation with author, January 2005.

9. Pablo Picasso. http://en.wikiquote.org/wiki/Pablo_Picasso.

10. Marcus Buckingham and Donald O. Clifton, *Now, Discover Your Strengths* (New York: The Free Press, 2001), 11.

11. Buckingham and Clifton, *Now, Discover Your Strengths,* 25.

12. Buckingham and Clifton, *Now, Discover Your Strengths,* 48.

13. Buckingham and Clifton, *Now, Discover Your Strengths,* 58.

14. Buckingham and Clifton, *Now, Discover Your Strengths,* 30.

15. G. K. Chesterton. www.twistedhistory.com/issues/may/0529.html#quotes.

16. John Eldredge. Quoting Howard Thurman at a Campus Crusade Christmas Conference in Denver, Colorado, January 2000.

17. Peter F. Drucker. Being interviewed by Jim Collins in *The Daily Drucker* (New York: HarperCollins, 2004), viii.

18. Jim Collins. Reflecting on his interview with Peter F. Drucker. *The Daily Drucker* (New York: HarperCollins, 2004), vii.

Chapter 4

1. Peggy Noonan. Sent in an e-mail to the author (Rick) but taken from *Forbes* magazine, September 14, 1992, 58.

2. This account is from "None So Blind" by Michael Shermer. *Scientific American,* February 9, 2004, www.sciam.com.

3. Attributed to Elton Trueblood. www.artsandfaith.com.

4. This story is often shared by Knofel Station who knows the family. Used with permission.

5. Thomas Huxley. Quoted in Karl Albrecht, *The Power of Minds at Work: Organizational Intelligence in Action* (New York: Amacon Books, 2002), 232.

6. Used with permission from the Miller family. (Twenty-six members of Lon Miller's family have died of ALS.)

Chapter 5

1. This account is from "American Anti Claims Silver." Associated Press article. www.sports.espn.go.com/oly/summer04/shooting/news/story?id=1864883.

2. Steve Sjogren. Quoted in Ted Haggard and Jack W. Hayford, *Loving Your City into the Kingdom* (Ventura, California: Regal Books, 1997), 134.

3. John Bruce. Personal conversation with the author. May 2003.

4. Tim Keller, *Ministries of Mercy: The Call of the Jericho Road* (Phillipsburg, New Jersey: P&R Publishing Company, second edition 1997), 212.

5. Keith Davy, *Passages: A Devotional Journey* (Orlando: WSN Press, 2004), 4.

6. Elton Trueblood. Quoted in Donald Atkinson, *Meeting Needs, Sharing Christ* (Nashville, Tennessee: LifeWay Press, 1995), 25–26.

7. Steve Sjogren, *Conspiracy of Kindness,* 23.

8. Lesslie Newbigin, *The Gospel in a Pluralistic Society* (Grand Rapids: Wm. B. Eerdmans Publishing Co., 1989), 132.

9. Mother Teresa, *Mother Teresa: In My Own Words.* Compiled by José Luis González-Balado (New York: Gramercy Books, 1996), 100.

10. Mother Teresa, *Mother Teresa: In My Own Words,* 100.

11. Robert G. Tuttle Jr., *Global Good News: Mission in a New Context.* Edited by Howard A. Snyder (Nashville, Tennessee: Abingdon Press, 2001), 176–189.

12. Eric Bryant. Conversation with author (Eric) in Los Angeles, California, September 15, 2005.

FORTUNE

1. Henry Cloud. *9 Things You Simply Must Do to Succeed in Love and Life* (Brentwood, Tennessee: Integrity Publishers, 2004), 41.

Chapter 6

1. Martin Luther King Jr. www.brainyquote.com/quotes/authors/m/martin_luther_king_jr.html.

2. Material in this section adapted from "Firefighters Appreciated" by Christophe Gontier, *The Bridge* magazine at LifeBridge Christian Church, Longmont, Colorado, November 2004, Vol. 4, Issue 4.

3. Material in this section adapted from "Remember to Breathe" by Dana Nelsen, *The Bridge* magazine at LifeBridge Christian Church, Longmont, Colorado, Summer 2002, Vol. 2, Issue 3.

4. Material in this section adapted courtesy of Paul S. Williams, *Laughter, Tears, and In-Between* (Cincinnati, Ohio: Standard Publishing, 2001), 126–128.

Chapter 7

1. Archimedes. http://www.everything2.com/index.pl?node=Archimedes.

2. Gladys Aylward. Quoted in Rit Nosotro, "Foreign Devil Turned Virtuous One," www.hyperhistory.net/apwh/bios/b3aylwardg.htm.

3. From a homily given by Fr. Shawn Hughes at Dunning Auditorium, Queen's University and St. Mary's Cathedral, Kingston, October 19, 2003. www.newmanhouse.ca/homily/motherteresa.html.

4. www.bible.org/illus.asp?topic_id=190.

5. George Sheehan. http://www.georgesheehan.com/welcome/bio.html.

6. Pope John Paul II. Quoted in Warren Bennis, "The Four Competencies of Leadership," *CIO* magazine, http://www.cio.com/executive/edit/chapter5.html.

7. Mother Teresa, *No Greater Love* (Novato, California: New World Library, 2002), 47.

8. Variously attributed to D. L. Moody, Billy Sunday, Martin Luther.

9. Peter Marshall. Quoted by Dr. Earl Palmer at First Presbyterian Church, Berkeley, California, 1971.

10. Mother Teresa, *Mother Teresa: In My Own Words.* Compiled by José Luis González-Balado (New York: Gramercy Books, 1996), 77.

Chapter 8

1. Bob Greene, *Once Upon a Town* (New York: HarperCollins, 2002), 14–15.

2. Bob Greene, *Once Upon a Town,* 151.

3. Rodney Stark, *The Rise of Christianity: How the Obscure, Marginal Jesus Movement Became the Dominant Religious Force in the Western World in a Few Centuries* (Princeton, New Jersey: Princeton University Press [arrangement with HarperCollins], 1996), 118.

4. FEMA official. Quoted by Jim and Jenny Key in conversation with author, September 2005.

5. From notes taken by author at church leaders' workshop. More info at www.justfaith.org.

6. Information and quotation in this section are from "Lost Boys Find Some Peace in U.S." by Mike Sandrock, April 25, 2004, www.boulderrunning.com/events/LostBoys.html.

7. Material in this section from an author (Eric) conversation with Gary Strudler, January 30, 2006.

8. Material in this section adapted from "Where Time Stands Still" by Joe Harvey, *The Bridge* magazine at LifeBridge Christian Church, Longmont, Colorado, Vol. 3, Issue 3.

9. Material in this section from an author (Eric) conversation with Kathy Greer at LifeBridge Christian Church, Longmont, Colorado, May 2004.

10. Material in section adapted from "Rock Bosnia" by Sheila Berg, *CCU514* magazine of Cincinnati Christian University, Spring 2006.

11. Peter F. Drucker, *Innovation and Entrepreneurship* (New York: HarperCollins, 1985), 21.

12. www.belay.org

ETERNITY

1. William Blake. www.brainyquote.com/quotes/quotes/w/williambla150123.html.

Chapter 9

1. "20th Century History," About, Inc., http://history1900s.about.com/library/weekly/aa042000a.htm.

2. Albert Schweitzer. http://www.sermonsplus.co.uk/Matthew%206.19-34.htm.

3. Hope for Bereaved, Inc., founded in 1978, is an independent, not-for-profit community organization in Syracuse, New York, dedicated to providing hope, support, and services for the bereaved. Hopeforbereaved.com.

4. Rick Warren, *The Purpose-Driven Life* (Grand Rapids, Michigan: Zondervan, 2002), 246.

5. Information in this section from an Associated Press article "More Than 1,000 Say Final Farewell to 'Daddy Bruce.'" No other data known.

6. Scott Berk, "Please Pass the Science—the Mysterious Leap Second," http://cardhouse.com/x13/x13science.htm.

7. "ERB Film News," Edgar Rice Burroughs, Inc., http://www.johncolemanburroughs.com/mag/1196.html.

8. "Jack La Lanne," Wikipedia article, http://www.answers.com/topic/jack-la-lanne.

9. Viktor Frankl. "Viktor Frankl," PBS, www.pbs.org/wgbh/questionofgod/voices/frankl.html.

Chapter 10

1. Anonymous. From The AgentZ, http://www.agentz.com/Inspiration/dash.html.

2. A. W. Tozer, *The Knowledge of the Holy* (San Francisco: HarperCollins, 1961), 1.

3. Glennice Harmon. Quoted by Academy of Achievement, "Basketball Coaching Legend" interview dated February 27, 1996, http://www.achievement.org/autodoc/page/woo0int-2.

4. Chris Lowney, *Heroic Leadership* (Chicago: Loyola Press, 2003), 212.

5. Chris Lowney, *Heroic Leadership,* 96.

6. Chris Lowney, *Heroic Leadership,* 29.

7. Chris Lowney, *Heroic Leadership,* 144.

8. Story courtesy Roger Hershey. Used with permission.

Reflections and Action Steps

Reflections and Action Steps

Reflections and Action Steps

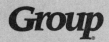